3-MINUTE TIPS
for
TEACHERS

3-MINUTE TIPS *for* TEACHERS

A Toolbox of Ideas for Teachers to Use the Entire School Year

HEATHER GARCIA
MICHELLE LINDSEY

ROWMAN & LITTLEFIELD
Lanham • Boulder • New York • London

Published by Rowman & Littlefield
An imprint of The Rowman & Littlefield Publishing Group, Inc.
4501 Forbes Boulevard, Suite 200, Lanham, Maryland 20706
www.rowman.com

86-90 Paul Street, London EC2A 4NE, United Kingdom

Copyright © 2022 by Heather Garcia and Michelle Lindsey

All rights reserved. No part of this book may be reproduced in any form or by any electronic or mechanical means, including information storage and retrieval systems, without written permission from the publisher, except by a reviewer who may quote passages in a review.

British Library Cataloguing in Publication Information Available

Library of Congress Cataloging-in-Publication Data
Names: Garcia, Heather, 1983– author. | Lindsey, Michelle, 1989– author.
Title: 3-minute tips for teachers : a toolbox of ideas for teachers to use the entire school year / Heather Garcia, Michelle Lindsey.
Other titles: Three-minute tips for teachers.
Description: Lanham, Maryland : Rowman & Littlefield, 2022. | Summary: "This book is filled with quick tips to help teachers through the school year. It is designed for the busy teacher"—Provided by publisher.
Identifiers: LCCN 2021055285 (print) | LCCN 2021055286 (ebook) | ISBN 9781475864069 (cloth) | ISBN 9781475864076 (paperback) | ISBN 9781475864083 (epub)
Subjects: LCSH: Teachers—Workload. | Classroom management. | Teacher–student relationships.
Classification: LCC LB2844.1.W6 G37 2022 (print) | LCC LB2844.1.W6 (ebook) | DDC 371.14/12—dc23/eng/20220124
LC record available at https://lccn.loc.gov/2021055285
LC ebook record available at https://lccn.loc.gov/2021055286

TABLE OF CONTENTS

Preface		ix
Introduction		1

Section 1: Preparing for the Start of School

1	Start Each Year Fresh	5
2	Know Your Standards before the School Year Begins	7
3	Open House Night	9
4	Setting Up Your Room	11
5	Don't Spend Your Check before You Earn It	15
6	Pre-School Nightmares	17

Section 2: Starting the School Year

7	Have Reasonable Expectations	21
8	Start Them Right into Content in an Engaging Way	23
9	Ice Breakers Are a Death Sentence	25
10	Accessing Online Platforms	27
11	Battling Cell Phones	29
12	Find Out Who the Friends Are and Move Them	31

Section 3: Making Your Workload More Manageable

13	Starting the Morning	35
14	Checking Email	37
15	Lesson Planning	39
16	Photocopies	41
17	Keeping Up with Grading	43
18	Build in Workdays	45
19	The Teacher Bag	47
20	Leaving for the Day	49
21	Stay Organized and Write Everything Down	51

Section 4: Establishing Student Routines

22	Collecting Student Work	55
23	Handing Back Student Work	57
24	Assigning Work	59
25	Behaviors Requiring Routines	61

Section 5: Dealing with Administration

26	Don't Panic when They Call (Or Email)	65
27	Informal Walk-Throughs	67
28	Formal Evaluations	69

Section 6: Communicating with Students, Parents, and Administration

29	Answering Emails	73
30	Calling Home	75
31	Using Mass-Text Alert Systems	77
32	Parent Conferences	79

Section 7: Optimizing Interpersonal Skills

33	Treat Your Students Like Rational Humans	83
34	Keep the Rules Simple	85
35	Chronically Absent Students	87
36	The Loud Kids	89
37	The Mean Kids	91
38	Choose Your Battles	93

Section 8: Thriving as an Educator

39	Choosing Your Work Tribe	97
40	Deciding Where You Eat Lunch	99
41	Know What You Can (and Cannot) Control	101
42	Using Your Time on Teacher Workdays	103
43	Ditch the Red Pen	105
44	What You Wear Matters	107
45	Good Teachers Are Always Students	109
46	Don't Let the Data Scare You	111
47	Polish Your Dragon Scales	113

Section 9: Increasing Student Engagement and Learning

48	Back to the Basics	117
49	Get 'em Movin'	119
50	Show Students the Work Means Something	121
51	Make It Yourself	123
52	Student Choice	125
53	Let Your Kids Struggle	127
54	Holy Sh*% Class Ended Early, Now What?	129

Section 10: Incorporating Reading and Writing

55	Reading Isn't Just for English Class	133
56	Get Them Writing	135

Section 11: Crossing the Digital Divide

57	Incorporating Technology	139
58	Let YouTube Help	141
59	Keep It PG	143

Section 12: Creating and Maintaining Your Work–Life Balance

60	Know Your Limits	147
61	Allow Yourself Time to Recharge	149
62	Know Your Contract	151
63	Censor Your Social Media	155
64	Don't Overshare with Your Students	157

Section 13: Ending the School Year

65	Don't Just Shove It All in a Box	161
66	Have Kids Help	163
67	Celebrate What Worked	165
68	Financially Surviving the Summer	169

For Further Reading	171
About the Authors	173

PREFACE

There are millions of teachers in the United States. Millions. Despite the physical distance between us, we want all teachers, new and veteran, elementary to secondary, regardless of discipline, to feel connected, to be inspired, and to ensure that at the end of the day, none of us *regret* the day. We don't want a single teacher to regret his or her decision to get into teaching. We cannot prevent this—but our hope is that through the practical advice in this book, this feeling will have a shorter lifespan. We want to help keep teachers teaching.

As fellow educators, we know not all days are going to be gold stars. They just aren't. That would be statistically impossible, right? Teachers have the same kids, at the same time, for the same class every day. Some days are bound to be better than others, regardless of how long we've been teaching.

There are ways to prepare, organize, and structure our professional lives to make these bad days happen less frequently, and that is what this book is for: to share the tools we've acquired from more than twenty-five years of combined teaching experience because we want to remind you that teaching is a mission. It isn't all about the good days. Those good days remind us why we became teachers all on their own. It's on those rough days, the days where we have to raise our voice or our lessons fall flat, that we have to remind ourselves why we do what we do. Let us help you help yourselves.

Think of what we are instructed to do when flying in an airplane—not that we fly often because let's be real, that's expensive—but everyone is instructed to save themselves before they save the little ones. The same principle applies: The school is the plane, we are the passengers, and our students are the helpless lumps we are responsible for saving.

Except, in the school, the airplane is being built while we are in the air flying and administrators throw jean-day coupons at us in their attempt to help while we try to secure enough oxygen to do what needs to be done. We have to keep ourselves healthy and well before we can properly enrich the minds of our students. Our hope is that this book will give teachers the fresh air that they so desperately need to survive. We are in this together because we're not robots, we're humans, and we shouldn't have to do it alone.

INTRODUCTION

This book is the peer teacher everyone *wishes* they had been assigned when they entered the profession and the refresher veteran teachers might be searching for later in their career.

But, teachers are busy. Really busy. Exhaustingly busy. We don't want this book to be *one more* thing that consumes your spare time. It is important to us that each chapter can be read independent of one another, in any particular order, and in short bursts, so if you need some quick tips on the fly, we want you to be able to find what you need and save the rest for another spare moment. The chapters are arranged chronologically to take you through the school year, but it doesn't need to be read that way. You get to read what will help in the moment.

Our shared decades' worth of teaching experiences have been melted down and forged into useful tools that can be shared quickly. The average adult can read approximately 300 and 200 words per minute, and that is enough for a quick recharge, which is why each chapter in this book is written to be between 600 and 750 words long. Just three minutes. Done.

Essentially, we want teachers to be able to enjoy reading a chapter a day while they wait in the parent pick-up line to pick up their own children (while parked—of course), or while they wait in the copy room for their chance at the photocopier. The point is, you can read this book in tiny snippets wherever you are. It is designed for a busy teacher. It's designed for you.

We also care deeply about our readers and encourage you to take ownership of this book. Make it yours. Annotate in the margins. Highlight helpful sections. Use tabs to mark chapters you want to read again. Fill in the charts. Answer the questions. This book could be a beautiful mess every time you read through it.

Section 1

PREPARING FOR THE START OF SCHOOL

One
START EACH YEAR FRESH

As teachers, there is something huge to look forward to. A countdown. Other occupations have ridiculous countdowns like twenty-four years left before retiring. Teachers only need to count down ten months. It's like growing a giant stress baby and the due date is always June.

However, as much as teachers look forward to summer, they anxiously anticipate the start of the new school year. Every new student, new lesson, new memory, and new adventure awaits. Maybe they'll actually take the field trip they've been dying to take. Maybe this year they'll keep their desks in groups, try more projects, or sponsor that club the kids have been bothering them about. Each year brings new opportunities.

Not only do lessons need to metamorphosize and transform from year to year, but a teacher's work space should transform too. Each year, add something to make your life that much easier. If papers crowded the desk all year—causing huge anxiety—then that should be the transformation the following year: find an organizational method that will solve this issue.

One year, maybe add that much-needed desk fan. The point is to reflect on everything that annoyed you the year prior and vow to fix some of those things in the upcoming school year because teachers have that ability to try again. And again.

If your space isn't doing it for you anymore, here are some tips to make it better:

- Switch up the decor. Take down those old bulletin boards and refresh the space to make it usable. Stick up some peel and stick dry-erase wallpaper so you can create more work space for your kids and get them out of their desks more often.
- Rearrange the furniture—like you would a room in your house. If you normally keep your desks in rows, try groups, try a horseshoe. Try moving your desk or podium, too.

- When all else fails, request a room change. It's like buying a new house! As much of a pain as it can be to pack up and move, the fresh space to go along with the fresh year can be . . . well . . . refreshing.
- Throw away old, tired lesson plans. While you are at it, throw away the lesson plans that flopped! Anything that brought you displeasure, within reason, get rid of it because if no one is forcing you to do it again next year, don't.

New school years are magical times as long as they are seen for what they are—fresh opportunities for excellence. Let everything that failed from the previous year go (like the cell phone policy that went up in flames by Christmas), and focus on how you can make the next year the best it can be.

It should not only be the best school year for you, but also for your kids. There's a controversial philosophy floating around academia about whether or not teachers should get the low-down on their future kids: while other teachers ask around about kids on their roster, why not refuse to partake? Maybe you don't want to know who has eighty-two referrals, or a bad attitude, or a weak work ethic because kids deserve a blank slate, a fresh start, as much as teachers do. And, why not tell your kids about your refusal to judge them based on years prior?

Open the school year by giving them the opportunity to tell you what they want you to know about them. What *they* want their first impression to be.

On the very first day, when students walk in, hand them an index card and tell them to write about the prompt on the board.

The prompt: *I wish my teacher knew. . . .*

Give them three to five minutes to write. Explain that no one will see these, their answers are only for you. It's amazing how brutally honest some kids are. Allow them to tell you what they want you to know, not what other teachers THINK you should know. Their answers will undoubtedly surprise you. Maybe, do the activity with them and let them in on a secret—what you wish students knew about you. This little activity gives teachers a powerful way to start each year, with relationship building.

Two
KNOW YOUR STANDARDS BEFORE THE SCHOOL YEAR BEGINS

Whether a teacher is new to the profession, teaching a new course, or looking to solidify their teaching practices, the first and most important step in preparing a classroom is knowing which standards are expected to be taught. Period. More important than decorating the classroom; more important than organizing the cabinets; more important than arranging desks—knowing the standards of the course is essential.

Open house nights occur early in the year in most school districts, but in some districts, this night occurs even before the school year begins. To prepare for this night, you will need to draft a syllabus explaining what your course is about and what students can expect to learn in the course. If you do not have a strong handle on the standards, you won't have the confidence to adequately answer parent questions or concerns as they arise. Knowing the standards of a course allows teachers, parents, and students to be on the same team regarding curricular expectations.

Also, as you think ahead to the quarter, semester, or school year and begin planning on a large-scale (more than just day to day), you need to be able to grasp how the standards connect with one another, how they progress, and how you can systematically teach them to your students in a logical and intentional way.

Once the students come and the days get filled with daily planning and grading and parent conferences and faculty meetings, it can leave teachers a little pinched for time—time that is necessary for deep-thinking and strategic unit planning. It is best to get some of this heavy lifting accomplished at the beginning of the year, allowing teachers to create a roadmap for the teaching needed throughout the year. None of this can happen on the fly.

One place to start creating this roadmap is to look at the end goal—what assessment is going to be required for students to pass this course? Is teaching to a test the reason most teachers went into the field? Most likely not. Is it the expectation from the state education departments? Pretty much. Students are expected to pass these tests and to do so on the first try. Teachers must ensure students are taught the skills they need to be successful on these standardized measurements. Therefore, teachers must know what is on these tests.

Most states will post their test item specifications on their department of education websites. This is a great place to start looking for which standards students will be assessed on at the end of the year and how heavily weighted they are. These should become your priority standards, the ones you teach first and most frequently throughout the year.

Think of these priority standards as weights in the gym. A student isn't going to lift the weight once and get strong. They might struggle in the beginning, require spotting (scaffolding), and then gain confidence to try it on their own. A student needs multiple repetitions of lifting that particular weight to build the muscle to do it with ease.

Ensuring these standards are the focus of the course will help to ensure students leave the class prepared not only for the exam at the end but also for the next courses in the sequence, setting them up for future success. But before that can happen, you must know what those standards say and how they provide the direction for your course.

As you work to master your standards and think about lesson planning for the year, you can reference the list below (and also reference the chapter on lesson planning):

1. Locate the test item specifications (sometimes called a test blueprint).
2. Make a list of all the standards that are being assessed.
3. List how heavily each of those standards is weighted.
4. Go into your standards and circle all the verbs and nouns of the standard to ensure you are clear on what the standard is asking students to be able to do.
5. Make a list of any discipline-specific vocabulary from the standards your students might struggle with and ensure you intentionally teach these words and meanings to students.
6. As you begin planning lessons, prioritize the list of standards that are assessed, ensuring the more heavily weighted standards are given priority.
7. As the year progresses, ensure that you are practicing those priority standards frequently and with a variety of materials.

Three
OPEN HOUSE NIGHT

Open house nightmares are common. Even veteran teachers have annual dreams of classrooms getting moved the day before parents come and boxes and file folders all over every surface, every cabinet is open. Chaos. Nightmares of chaos. Dreams of coming on the wrong night or forgetting to wear shoes or any variation of this nightmare is normal. Are the fears unwarranted? Most likely. Does it stop the nightmares? Usually not. There is even an entire chapter of this book dedicated specifically to teacher nightmares.

Most teachers get into the field because of the kids and the content—the parents are a necessary add-on causing newbies and veterans alike nervous tics. Adults are pretty much the worst. Some adults can be critical and questioning, and if you don't have yourself prepared for this night in the right way, these parents will notice.

The temptation of new teachers is sometimes to have the room 100%, Pinterest and Instagram ready: every bulletin board filled, every bauble and banner in place, the calendar for the month all filled in, etc. Having your room look like a showroom is a lovely goal, but certainly isn't the most important part of open house night.

Parents will want to get a general feel for your room as an extension of yourself. Is it tidy (are you tidy?). Is there a purpose and a flow (have you been thoughtful about how their child will function in the space?) Are class items broken or vandalized? These all matter to parents, and kids.

Pinterest-ready rooms don't matter. Tidy rooms do. Beyond having the room ready, all teachers, whether they teach kindergarten or seniors, will need to come up with a plan for dealing with parents on parent night. It is best to have a quick slide deck ready to show parents or a handout of highlights such as:

- the academic objectives of your course
- your supply list
- your contact information

Parents come to open house night to hear what you have to say, to put a face to the teacher, and to get a feel for their child's learning environment.

Even if open house happens before your students begin school, it is important to know who your kids with learning accommodations are. If a student has a vision impairment or hearing difficulties, that student might need to sit toward the front of the room, and you should have a plan before open house night. These parents will wait to talk to you alone. Guaranteed.

Before the parents come for open house night, if you are an elementary school teacher, prepare a seating chart with nameplates on the desks so kids know where their seats will be (assuming school hasn't started yet). Having their names labeled in bright colors, laminated, and taped to the desk with sparkly tape isn't necessary. A bright post-it note on the desk with their name on it will do the job.

If you are a secondary teacher, the seating chart isn't nearly as important on parent night. These parents aren't as concerned with seeing the actual seat their child will sit in as much as they care about the content their child will be learning and the teacher they will be learning it from.

In the chart below there are some quick dos and don'ts for you to consider as you prepare for open house.

Table 3.1

Open House Quick-Guide	
Do	Don't
<ul><li>Wear comfortable shoes (you will be doing SO much standing and walking).</li><li>Wear a shirt that won't highlight sweat.</li><li>Wear nice fitting clothes.</li><li>Keep accessories and nail polish understated.</li><li>Have a handout for parents—they want to leave with something in their hands.</li><li>Have the room tidy (even if it means shoving boxes under your desk to hide them).</li><li>Have a welcome message on your board.</li><li>Have places for people to sit with clean surfaces.</li><li>Know your standards before tonight so you can answer questions.</li><li>Play instrumental music softly in the background.</li></ul>	<ul><li>Wear uncomfortable shoes.</li><li>Wear uncomfortable or revealing clothes.</li><li>Have chipped nail polish.</li><li>Wear a T-shirt (unless all the teachers were told to wear a specific shirt for open house night).</li><li>Feel compelled to spell out every minute of every day for parents. They just need an overall gist.</li><li>Waste time filling in every single bulletin board.</li><li>Leave boxes around or leave your desk a mess.</li><li>Feel the need to have a special theme to your handouts, keep it simple.</li></ul>

Four
SETTING UP YOUR ROOM

If teachers are lucky enough to have a choice in the matter, how they arrange their classroom can be a difficult decision.

Choose wisely.

It might depend on the type of classes you will be teaching that year, what kind of assignments you want to incorporate, or what kind of vibe you want to have.

There are many options depending on if you have long rectangle tables, single person desks, round tables for four, science lab tables, etc. And, as most teachers know, there are pros and cons to both of the following.

Rows (table 4.1)

Table 4.1

Pros	Cons
• Everyone faces forward toward the board • Minimizes distractions • Easier to create seating charts and separate those students who most definitely need to be separated • Teachers can see most, if not all, students while at the front of the room • Students get excited if they are rearranged for one day for group activities and tend to take them more seriously	• Not conducive to group work • Not always conducive to student participation. Meaning, kids tend to be less vocal in a setting so formal • Easier for kids to cheat off one another • Might create smaller pathways for walking

CHAPTER FOUR

Groups (table 4.2)

Table 4.2

Pros	Cons
• Group discussions can happen more easily and spontaneously • Shared brain power can be meaningful • Harder to cheat when they only have one peer next to them (and, let's be real, who probably doesn't know the right answer as well)	• Classroom noise (chatter) tends to be higher • Group work loses its excitement if done too often • Harder to see all students as some of their backs might be to you (not the board—make sure they can always see the board) • Easier to hide their phones—for sure

Both setups have their merits. Whichever route you choose, here are some tips to make either route easier to navigate:

- If in rows, give the kids a shoulder partner. Instead of separating all the desks into single rows, organize them by two. Thicker rows with two desks touching will help with any impromptu collaboration you might want and will open up walkways.
- In groups, make sure you assign the seats. They will always, always, sit in a pod made up of their friends. This is bad. Very bad.
- In groups, make a new seating chart every few weeks so students get comfortable working with different students.
- If in groups, make sure every student can see the board.
- With either setup, make sure there's a seat for administrators. Whenever you get those walk-throughs, always make sure there is an empty seat by the door and only place excellent students near that empty seat—students who always know what's going on and won't let you down because you can guarantee an administrator will ask that student some questions about the lesson that day.

Setting up your room doesn't only entail how your desks are arranged though. You will have wall decor, bulletin board displays, and board space.

Some schools might dictate what needs to be displayed on your boards. Some schools want word walls, objectives, daily agendas, etc., displayed for kids at all times. If so, no worries. Invest in some colorful cute tape that can be easily removed without damaging your boards. Devote a section of your board to these requirements. If you teach several different courses, here's how you can set up your board using decorative tape as your section dividers (table 4.3).

SETTING UP YOUR ROOM   13

Table 4.3

Class:	Class:	Class:	Class:
Objective:	Objective:	Objective:	Objective:
Daily Agenda:	Daily Agenda:	Daily Agenda:	Daily Agenda:
Homework:	Homework:	Homework:	Homework:

If you only teach two classes, you can have room for important announcements and/or due dates (table 4.4).

Table 4.4

Class:	Important Announcements and Due Dates:	Class:
Objective:		Objective:
Daily Agenda:		Daily Agenda:
Homework:		Homework:

You can dedicate one of your bulletin boards as a place to submit exit tickets. Label the board "Exit Tickets" and stick thirty push pins into the board. Then, when students complete exit tickets on index cards, sticky notes, or scrap pieces of paper, they can tack up their ticket on their way out of class. It might be easier to keep track of these tickets so those tiny slips of paper don't get lost in other piles of work.

Make sure your room is functional for you and your kids. Don't dedicate a bulletin board to a word wall if you have no intention of updating it. Make the space work and make sure it's functional.

Five
DON'T SPEND YOUR CHECK BEFORE YOU EARN IT

Setting up a classroom can be *expensive*. Especially if you are a social media maven who enjoys a good Pinterest board or Instagram account. Some of these teachers seem to have money to spare, and they spare no expense. Please understand, this is NOT the expectation—especially of beginning teachers. At *no point* should you be considering taking out a credit card to purchase paper balls to hang from a ceiling (those are a fire hazard by the way). At *no point* should you be using bill money or money from savings to purchase matching bins to hold your centers.

Here's the deal—kids don't care. They want their materials contained, sure. But a spray-painted cardboard shoe box or flimsy plastic one-dollar bin will be sufficient. They don't care about brands or farmhouse chic. Organizing your space is a must. Decorating your space to perfection right out of the gate is not.

Here is a list of what you might want to consider having in your room as you set it up:

- Desk organizer for your sticky notes, pens, notepads, and other quick-grab essentials
- File folders and hanging files or a binder to keep your important documents in (People usually prefer one method to the other.)
- An inflatable beach ball for class discussions and activities (Seriously. They are inexpensive, they don't hurt when they get thrown, and they increase engagement.)
- If you are an elementary teacher who inherited a classroom full of centers and books and resources (YIPEE!) organizing those is going to be a must. You cannot teach from what you don't understand, so you may need to repurpose some old boxes to sort, store, and organize.
- Cover ugly boards. Usually, there is somewhere on campus to find large bulletin board paper. If not, a cheap roll of wrapping paper will do the trick. The idea is to decorate the space to make your heart happy but not break the bank.

- Clean surfaces. If the desks are covered in writing and you want a clean slate, a few heavy-duty cleaning sponges might be in order (my favorite are the Magic Erasers or similar products). Kids who enter a dirty space are less likely to care if they add to the mess. A tidy space lends itself to further tidiness.

If you feel like this isn't enough, the kids need more (or you need more), you can always look other places for ways to make your room appealing, and it doesn't all need to be brand new.

- Start within your school. Ask the teachers on your team if they have any decorations or leftover borders they are willing to donate to your cause. Chances are, they will have some.
- If you have a dollar store in your area (not the brand name, but a store that sells its items for one dollar) there is usually a teacher section appearing around July. Try looking there for some awesome deals! Their plastic drinking cups are great for sorting pencils and markers too.
- DonorsChoose.org is a website where you can place your requests within the platform and donors will scroll through the website looking for people and projects to donate money to. A nicely written explanation and some pictures can go a long way. I have seen teachers walk away with full class sets of new novels from the generosity of donors on Donors Choose. Just make sure you aren't just asking for pretty things. Ensure what you ask for affects learning.

At the end of the day, kids want a clean, organized, safe space. If it is pretty, fine, but don't start spending money on your room until you have *actually* started earning money. No teacher should go into debt just to set up their classroom.

Six
PRE-SCHOOL NIGHTMARES

These are real. These are *so* real. For weeks before the beginning of a new school year, many teachers are plagued with nightmares that make sleep an unfathomable, imaginary concept. Waking up in an instant panic because they think they're two hours late for the first day of school even though the first day of school might still be twenty-two days out.

Dreams are obviously just subconscious insecurities, right? The imposter syndrome is flying its flag high and proud regardless of how knowledgeable you are in your content area. These insecurity dreams can manifest in multiple fashions:

- It will be the first day of school with kids, only . . . you didn't know or didn't realize and you show up in leggings or basketball shorts like you would for a Professional Development Day.
- You oversleep on the first day of school and are late to your first hour.
- You show up on the first day and everything you own and have neatly tucked away has actually exploded onto every desk surface in your room and your kids are bound to walk in any minute. Yeah, this one is a doozy. File folders, beach balls for discussions, textbooks, everything just exploded onto desks like academic shrapnel.
- The first day is absolute and complete anarchy. The kids are heathens. Foaming at the mouth, refusing to listen, moving around the room. Wild. Animals.
- This one, and this one is the most frequent, none of your lesson plans are ready. Not a single photocopy, not a single idea regarding any sort of plan.
- Do you have shoes on? Probably not. Your classroom could be in flames, and you don't have shoes.

Teachers are not imposters. However, feeling like they will be inadequate on that first day, a day where first impressions are so important, just will not go away. Year after year teachers have these dreams. Regardless of two, seven, or fifteen years of teaching, precious sleep has been lost over these dreams that aren't that farfetched from reality. These things could happen. There could have been a water leak and custodians had to empty cabinets to clean up water. It. Could. Happen. Teachers could accidentally flake out and confuse the start day with a Teacher Work Day. Or, and even worse, kids could be completely uncontrollable.

That is where the fear lies: in the possibility that the metaphorical sh*t could hit the fan (or even literal, you just never know). However, because there is this overwhelming anxiety that these possibilities could actually happen, use these dreams as premonitions and over prepare. Use these fears as preparation tools.

The fear of oversleeping can be overcome by setting twelve alarms. Spouses love this. The fear of wearing workout clothes can be combated by picking out your outfit the night before, AND, trying it on because there's nothing worse than thinking you have everything figured out only to find out that dress or those pants haven't fit you in like three years.

Because of those dreams, teachers will never be without lesson plans on the first day. Dreams serve as cautionary tales. The moment teachers return to their rooms, they are prepping for the first day. And, students will never be wild animals because teachers know their expectations and they know how to lay those out for the kids. Teachers know these things and, if they're new, they learn quickly. Teachers know how to begin the year.

Just know, you are not alone in experiencing those dreams that ruin the few peaceful moments you have remaining in your summer break. These are normal. And, they show you you care. You care about first impressions and you care about starting the year right. These nightmares happen not because you are imposters, but because you might be perfectionists. There's a huge difference.

Section 2

STARTING THE SCHOOL YEAR

Seven
HAVE REASONABLE EXPECTATIONS

The point of creating goals is to reach them, right? So why set yourselves up for goals that cannot be achieved? If, and really it should say "when," administration asks you for predictions on state exams, what do you say? Do you say you predict a 60% pass rate? What about the other 40%? It might not sit right to discount the efforts of those who might not make the cut, but you can't very well say 100%. No one can predict those kinds of results.

What if one of your students needs to poop? Seriously. What if some kid with a shy tummy who refuses to poop in school needs to poop during their two hour exam. It happens. Their tummy issues are in no way a reflection of your teaching but if you promise a 100% pass rate and only deliver 82% because lots of kids had to poop, then what?

When setting expectations for test scores, you have to keep them realistic. Teachers want their kids to do well, it's natural. However, not everyone shows up ready to play ball on testing day, and you need to account for that. Some of those grade predictions might go higher than your school principal. They might go to the district leadership team. Those numbers need to be genuine predictions, not hopes. And, you shouldn't feel guilty about that 30% who might not make it.

If it helps, offer various statistics, like a menu. Option One: Pass vs. fail. This one seems harsh but gets the job done. Option Two: Confident pass vs. possible pass (with proper motivation) vs. unlikely to pass. This way, you have a little wiggle room in your predictions. For example: 65% should most definitely pass, 20% could pass if the conditions are right, and 15% are still performing below where they need to be. This data sounds less harsh.

Teacher expectations extend beyond testing though. Each year, with your fresh start, you get to set new goals for yourself too and this doesn't just mean testing scores. These goals could be work-life balance, organization, classroom management, etc.

Goals should reflect where you live within your teaching career. Is it your first year teaching? Know what your goal should be? Survival. Nothing more is expected of you—at least it shouldn't be. Survive, come back, and thrive later. An attainable goal for a new teacher? Don't let the heathens see you cry. That's attainable.

Veteran teachers' egos are a little less sensitive and a student probably hasn't made them cry (negatively) in about a thousand years. They are immune to their childish deflecting. Their expectations for themselves should probably have shifted from when they were fresh, brand new, wrinkle free teachers trying to survive and should probably be focused more on personal or professional growth. But, some types of growth require time, patience, reflection, and possibly some reassessing. This long-term growth might not happen as quickly as you want. So be it. Count the little steps you made as a success.

Expectations and goals are best met when teachers narrow them down and limit them. Not lower them, because, well, yeah, that would be much easier. Set a few goals for your kids and a few for yourself. These need to be attainable, suitable, and significant, but not so significant that they can't reasonably happen within the time frame you're given.

Maybe set goals for your kids that don't revolve around numbers. If those goals are never met because they're too lofty or too unpredictable, because let's face it, teachers have zero control once kids enter the testing room, try a different goal-setting approach. Try leaning more toward engagement because teachers cannot control how many absences a student has, and they certainly can't control how many kids pass the state exam because too many factors play into the magical formula for success. But, engagement can happen. Maybe your goal is to include at least ten more activities that get kids out of their seats or the classroom.

When you are setting your goals for each school year, don't let anyone bulldoze you into thinking success equals a 100% pass rate. Instead, offer a percentage of growth. Attainable goals help prevent burnout. Nothing makes teachers feel more like failures or frauds than goals that weren't achieved, regardless if they were ever achievable in the first place. Set goals that mean something to you. Set goals that not only benefit your kids' growth, but also your personal growth.

Eight
START THEM RIGHT INTO CONTENT IN AN ENGAGING WAY

Setting the tone for a new school year is essential. It is important to set rules and routines. It is important to ensure students understand the climate of their classroom and get to know their peers. It is important to learn your kids' names and to ensure your kids feel seen and appreciated in your room. It is important to establish yourself as structured, fair, and knowledgeable. This all matters greatly. And it can all occur while diving right into content at the start of the year.

Most school years are around 190 days long. Once the necessary timewasters are removed, such as school pictures and assemblies and substitutes and professional development days and fire drills and progress monitoring and state testing, there are around 140 days of teaching available.

Every child has the right to end the school year knowing more than they did when they started it, and for this purpose alone, there is no time to waste on ice breakers (see the chapter on ice breakers). There isn't time to waste an entire class period going over the syllabus. Many schools and teachers have established climates of suspended curriculum at the beginning of the year in an attempt to teach routines and structures and study skills. This is admirable and important work, but it can be done in conjunction with teaching content.

In elementary schools, there is a little more time to perhaps go over schedules and routines—kindergarteners are just slightly larger pre-K kiddos, and they might need a little time to learn how to function in a classroom—but they can learn those essential skills while also learning how to write their letters and learn phonemes. In secondary classrooms, there are usually between forty and fifty minutes on average to teach them what they need to know to propel them forward in the curriculum. When it can be controlled, wasting an entire class period should not happen.

Some ways to dive right into content while still teaching routines, getting kids to know their peers, and establishing classroom structures includes partnering students up and giving them a bite-sized task to complete relating to content (eg. in sixty seconds, circle every noun you find in this opening to a short story; in five minutes, solve as many of these word problems as you can; in eight minutes, label the parts of this sunflower).

Then, have the students partner with another set of partners near them to share their results. Kids are working together, with content, and breaking down social barriers through teamwork. Have students work with each other so they learn names and develop comfort, but don't make them present to the whole class on day one. That would just be mean.

Adding a developmentally appropriate timed component to tasks establishes routines of not wasting time, diving right into the assignment, and setting a fast and exciting pace for the class. At the end of the activity, show students the routines for turning in work and have them follow the routine, then dive into another short-burst assignment. Hand students new colored pencils to complete color-coding activities and then, before putting them away, explain the procedure for doing so. Students don't need to be lectured on all of the rules and routines right away on day one, teach them as they come up.

Since reviewing a syllabus and reviewing course expectations is important, rather than dedicate long chunks of time to these activities, use these documents to teach skills needed within your course such as active reading and annotation. Teach kids how to mark up the text in a meaningful way. Send students on a scavenger hunt through the document to find words they don't know. Keep the pace fast, keep the kids working, and keep them engaged in content from day one.

Nine
ICE BREAKERS ARE A DEATH SENTENCE

Do you know what happens in a class with twenty-five or more kids who know each other well, talk to each other often, and are comfortable with one another? Chaos. In an environment where laws of the animal kingdom already run rampant and teachers must assert their alpha status on a daily basis, do they really want all the kids to be friends right away? Absolutely not.

Do not feel the need to put your kids into teams of four to see who can stack the plastic cups the fastest using a rubber band and four pieces of string to yank and pull. No. No way.

Understand the importance of classroom management. An atmosphere is set within those first few weeks of school, and it is up to the teacher to decide what kind of atmosphere is created. Would an icebreaker work in a class like ROTC where camaraderie and team building is essential? Absolutely. They do not need camaraderie right away in English II or Algebra I.

Having fun in the classroom is important for learning. This is known. You may eventually break out the rubber bands and cups before completing your first group project, and this is great, but give it a month, maybe even two before unleashing this chaos because, if you do it too soon, it's really hard to come back from it.

However, the complete opposite is also true. Don't feel the need to humdrummingly go over the classroom syllabus for the entire forty-five-minute class period. If you force them to sit there while you hammer home every classroom procedure and rule then that is also not the atmosphere you want to create. Teachers typically want students to like their class and want them to feel excited to be there, but they don't need a relay race balancing eggs on spoons while being guided blindfolded by a partner to do this. And, they certainly don't need to learn three things about the person sitting next to them and then report out. Gross.

After a day like this—a day full of icebreakers, chatter, laughing, movement—how are you supposed to switch gears and get into something solitary or more subdued? How can you switch from cup stacking to essay writing without sending your students mixed signals?

There's a balance that can be struck. You can get to know your kids without having them march around your room to play people bingo. Do not let them get out of their chairs! Especially, and this is said with so much love, if you are a teacher who struggles with classroom management. Classroom management is an ever-evolving concept. As kids become comfortable throughout the year, they will push and stretch your expectations. They'll soon try to get up and move around to show their friend their phone, steal a snack, etc. If your class is not the place for any of this, then don't promote that free moving behavior on the very first day.

Instead, in order to get to know your kids, you might play a game of Would You Rather? You can learn more about them as humans because building relationships with students is just as important as creating a certain atmosphere. But, instead of having them run to one side of the room or the other to decide, have them write or type their response. Then, ask for some to share. You will still get giggles, kids are still engaged, but it's controlled. It's the illusion of fun.

And, what about your shy students? You will have those kids who would rather fail a project than present the content. Those kids do not want to get up and start interviewing their peers about their hobbies. They don't. By catering to the few who are outgoing enough to do that, you are forcing so many others to shut down. Choose something inclusive, but not intrusive. Keep the tone light on the first day but choose something that doesn't, and probably shouldn't, promote and encourage behavior you would be appalled to see in the middle of a lesson.

And, if you are a veteran teacher and you absolutely refuse to give up your ice breakers because they work for you, then so be it. But please, please, quit encouraging brand new teachers to do these on the first day of school. It's sometimes impossible to undo this damage.

Ten

ACCESSING ONLINE PLATFORMS

When teachers and students all over the country had to dive into online learning with little to no transition time, many school districts were thrown into chaos. Learning was suspended for multiple weeks while teachers learned to switch their curriculums to an online delivery system or Learning Management System (LMS).

Students as young as four years old needed to be taught how to dive into these online platforms to access their content. Parents needed to be taught how to support their children as this transition to online learning happened. Students and teachers were connecting through video chats and navigating new online challenges.

It was a messy but necessary process. Thankfully, everyone knows better now.

The lesson educational institutions from across the world learned was unprecedented: the world needs to be prepared to "go virtual" in an instant. This means the way content and technology is introduced to kids needs to have intentional procedures.

At the beginning of the school year, perhaps toward the end of the first week of school, teach students how to log into their online learning management system (and have them bookmark it in their browser). Have them complete a quick content-based assignment they can find success with. Understand students might be frustrated with the online system already, so an easier task will give them a feeling of accomplishment, and by using content to bring them onto the platform, you can walk students through how to turn in assignments and where to find their grades.

Engaging students in an online discussion early in the year provides the opportunity to establish classroom norms regarding online protocols and expectations. Students may be accustomed to the lack of rules in the online world of social media, so establishing the rules for classroom-based online discussion may stave off future problems. Look to your school's code of conduct and remind students that the consequences for breaking rules in person also apply to breaking rules in an online space. Teachers cannot assume students automatically internalize this reality.

Teachers should also never assume a student knows how to, or remembers how to use the online platform. At the start of the year, give every student a level playing field by walking them through this crucial step. Even after the year progresses, students need to log in to their LMS systems regularly so they develop a comfort level strong enough to carry them through independent online learning if students ever need to engage in virtual learning in the future. Students learn through repetition, and so do teachers.

Teachers need to be comfortable with the online platforms districts have provided so they can switch curriculum online if the need arises. This will require practice. Logging in once at the beginning of the year to set up a teacher page and then abandoning it won't provide any level of comfort.

This doesn't mean all of the lessons need to live in an online space. This doesn't mean everything needs to be replicated both in-person and online. It means, as teaching and learning evolve, teachers and students evolve alongside it.

Some teachers have dived right into online platforms and will never go back. Their entire curriculum is digital, and they are loving the transition. Some teachers prefer the paper and pencil route, and no amount of enhanced technology will sway them. Neither approach is wrong. However, it is the educator's responsibility to ensure students are prepared to access their materials online. The best way to ensure this happens is to establish a routine allowing students to access their online platform regularly.

Some ways to accomplish this might include:

- Create Monday check-ins where students type a quick blurb about their weekend in an online platform as a warm-up when they walk in the room.
- If a quiz is going to be multiple-choice, have them complete it on the online learning management system rather than with paper and pencil. (Chances are, the Learning Management System will grade it for you.)
- Create an online notebook where students can keep track of their vocabulary. Slide decks work great as virtual flashcards—especially if you have students use animation to have the definitions or examples appear on the screen after the initial term or phrase. This slide deck can live in their learning management system for easy access.
- Once a month have students read an article from an online resource you place into their learning management system, then have them complete a discussion with their peers for homework.

Eleven

BATTLING CELL PHONES

When most teachers were in school, they did not have a cell phone. Why? Because cell phones didn't really exist. Once texting became a thing, it was exhausting because you had to hit the number 1, three times to get the letter "C."

That is not the case today and there is no magic formula to make this wide-spread cell phone distraction, perhaps even addiction, disappear. Students have endless access to the world around them and it's hard to get them to zero in on what's going on within your four walls when they could know what's going on in someone's life in another country. So, what do you do?

- *Scenario One:* You could implement a no phone policy. A hard no-phone policy. Good luck. They will just sneak them. It's not as simple as that. They will prop open their textbooks or laptops, slip their phones into them, and continue to do whatever they feel like doing.

    It will be an endless battle, daily. And, what's the punishment when you do find it out, because you will? Take it? That's a quick way to ruin relationships. They see it as a personal attack on their souls when their phones are taken away.
- *Scenario Two:* You collect them. We've all probably seen those ambitious teachers who buy shoe racks and number the slots and make students place their phones in the slots before attendance will be taken. Guess what, some of those phones are decoys. Some phones cost hundreds of dollars and their entire lives are in the device. They don't care about attendance, those aren't their real phones they put into the shoe rack. Plus, do you really want to be responsible if someone grabs the wrong phone on the way out?
- *Scenario Three:* And, this might actually work. Some teachers set up charging stations. Students will separate from their phones if new life is being breathed into them. But, the phones have to be in sight. If you try to put the station in a closet or something it won't work. They won't fall for it. However, if the station is near them,

they will feel inclined to check it. Instead, maybe put the station behind your desk. It isn't a convenient enough place for them to walk over and loiter. Just make it a rule, if they charge it, it lives there for the class period, or something.

- *Scenario Four:* And, this works most of the time: allow students to use their phones once a class period. They get one shot to check their phone or send a quick text. One. It sounds like it would be hard to keep track of but it really isn't. Students see the respect being shown toward their lives outside the classroom. They have social drama, jobs, families, etc. They need their phones on them just like teachers do. Sort of. At least, they think so anyway.

Whichever path you decide, make sure it doesn't violate any district policy. And, make sure whatever your personal policy is, detail it in your syllabus. If it's in the syllabus, which parents are encouraged to read, then it makes defending your choices that much easier.

Never. Ever. Snatch a kid's phone out of their hands. So many issues can result from this. What if you drop it? Scratch the student? Accidentally miss and smack them in the face?

Anything could go wrong with this. Once students violate the one time rule (which they do because they're kids), have them personally prop it up on a bookshelf behind your desk. By propping it, they can still see it and be comforted in knowing it's still there. Plus, it isn't really a fight to get them to do it. They had their warning, it was acknowledged. There's usually a joke about if it was worth it and they usually reply honestly. They get it back when the bell rings and there isn't too much drama involved.

Who knew this was the technological route classes were heading? However, this new battle is not something you will win with antiquated discipline techniques. Teachers have to be just as crafty with their discipline as the kids are with hiding their phones. Teachers need to preserve as much learning as possible without sabotaging student–teacher relationships in the process.

Twelve

FIND OUT WHO THE FRIENDS ARE AND MOVE THEM

Oh my goodness, move the friends. *You* are not friends with these kids. You might hurt their feelings by shifting their axis of comfort away from beloved besties. You need to protect the learning environment in your room. Those friends *can't* be near each other. If you set up your room alphabetically and two students with the last name of Smith have been sitting side by side since kindergarten, then guess what, those kids are friends. Perhaps not besties that go to movies on the weekends, but they will talk. Why? Familiarity breeds chatter. Plain and simple.

Move them.

It is best to let kids know, right up front, on day one of school, that you have already chosen their seats.

It is also best to assign their seats before they EVER sit down.

Students are creatures of comfort and creatures of habit. If the kids go through the trouble of choosing their seats, unpacking their stuff, lining up their pens, setting their water bottle in JUST the right spot, and then you start class and ask them to stand so you can assign them seats, you have LOST them. They are grumpy. They are slamming things in their bags. They are displeased. That is not the tone to set on the first day of school (or any day of school).

Instead, spend a few minutes the day before and, using Post-It Notes, write each child's first name and last initial. Then, right before class starts, run around and put the post-it notes down on the desks. Run like a mad person. It should take less than a minute to slap a post-it on each desk. Have them pre-organized by class period. Then, on day one when the students come in, tell them to find their names and take a seat (it helps if you give them something to quietly work on while they wait for you to come in).

DO NOT let them walk around and chat with friends. Then they are grumpy when you ask them to sit. Have them sit right down and get to work at the seat YOU chose for them.

Don't bother with the seating chart yet. Wait. Once you see who the friends are, and once you move them, THEN make your chart so you can start memorizing names.

Even once you make your first seating chart, here is a word of advice: watch for the kids who walk in together. Those children waited for each other before they came to your room (safety in numbers). Separate them.

Peek down the hall as the couples come walking up. If they were holding hands a few minutes ago, split them up. Perhaps not on day one, but on day two for certain. Shake them *all* up so nobody feels singled out, but seriously, they can't be near each other. They will whisper and distract each other and in turn, distract you and those around them. If they get into arguments, which they will, the imposed close quarters will distract them AND you. Their tense body language will scream almost as loudly as their real argument might.

Later (much later), when everyone is comfortable with each other and you have memorized all of their names, choosing their seats can be a reward that students work toward. But if you start off letting them choose their own seats, there is no carrot, there is nothing to dangle. Kids will move MOUNTAINS to sit next to their friends, so they can certainly move a class average of 62% to a class average of 75% if they *really* want to. But when you are first starting the year and establishing rules and routines, MOVE THOSE FRIENDS.

Section 3

MAKING YOUR WORKLOAD MORE MANAGEABLE

Thirteen
STARTING THE MORNING

In a school, the bell reigns supreme. It signals the start and end of the day. At a secondary school, they signal when class begins and when it ends. They signal when teachers have a moment to use the restroom, when they get to eat, and when they get a blissful forty to fifty minutes to themselves where they can hopefully make it to the copier, grade some papers, and write lesson plans. Teachers are at the mercy of the clock. There isn't much they get to control. It is essential, in those blissful minutes before the students arrive and the bell begins ringing, they seize control of this part of the day.

Creating a morning routine catered around your exact needs can make your mornings run more smoothly. Some important routines to establish include:

- *Change the date on your board.* Seriously, this gets forgotten. Often.
- *Write your daily objectives on the board along with other information you need students to know* (such as test dates, homework, etc.).
- *Prioritize your emails.* There may be important school announcements or communication from parents you need to know before the day begins, and clearing out email first thing in the morning can feel liberating. There is a chapter dedicated specifically to answering emails.
- *Ensure you have the materials you need for the day ready and organized.* Do you need scissors, tape, a set of books, chart paper, markers? If you are scrambling to gather these items together, when the time arises and you need them, you are wasting educational time for your students. Have these items easy to access at the start of the day.
- *Tidy the desks.* They always seem to creep forward by the end of the day; reclaim your space at the front of the room. It also gives you a chance to check for graffiti and to clean it off before the day begins.
- *Set up your technology.* Sometimes technology inexplicably does not work. If you can eliminate *that* roadblock and troubleshoot before the students arrive, you can preserve educational time and eliminate the stress of coming up with a backup lesson when you discover the tech failure.

There are some places, and people, you should avoid in the mornings. Try not to spend too much time in the copy room. It can cause undue stress, especially around exam times when the photocopier is in high demand—and it will ALWAYS break when you need it, thus heightening the stress.

Any space where teachers gather in the morning is most likely not a place you want to be.

Sometimes teachers, without meaning to, can be a little grouchy or complaining in the mornings, and *that* is the worst way to begin a day. Try to surround yourself with positive energy in the mornings, and the copy room or the mailroom is usually not the place to find it.

Try to preserve this morning time as much as possible. Even if you have a best friend in the room next door, resist the urge to spend the morning catching up unless your room and your board are completely ready. A frazzled morning can lead to a frazzled day, and having your board and your lesson ready can lead to a smoother day for both you and your students.

If you have a morning duty preventing any of this from occurring, then your after-school routine is going to include many of these items so you don't have a hectic start to your day.

Keep in mind, there will be days you are running late, or an unexpected parent meeting came up, or a fellow teacher was talking your ear off and you couldn't get away. Those mornings happen to everyone. But if you can control as many of your mornings as possible, you will find the day will run more smoothly, which hopefully will make you a happier teacher with happier students. Morning routines may seem like a silly ritual, but they do have the power to change your day and ultimately, your year.

Fourteen

CHECKING EMAIL

Establishing a healthy routine as a teacher takes time and intention, but it is *easy* to fall into bad habits, especially surrounding the issue of emails.

Here are the cardinal rules for email routines: do not check your email from your phone. Or on weekends. Or on holidays. Period.

Unless your school district pays for your cell phone, it exists for *your* convenience, not the school's, not the parents', and not even the kids'.

Teachers need boundaries, otherwise, like a giant multi-tentacled Kraken from the deep, this job will steal away every morsel of your time if you allow it. This is because, in education, the work is never "done." Just when you think every paper has been graded, guess what, the kids work some more. Just when every email has been answered, another comes in. Just when every parent contact has been made, another parent wants a follow-up. The work never ends, therefore, you must establish boundaries so you do not become a twenty-four-hour teacher. Teaching is your career, not your entire life.

Now granted, you might think about teaching constantly, sometimes this is an unavoidable symptom of teaching—especially as the start of the year draws near. But if you choose to daydream about the first days of school and how you want to rearrange your desks, *that* is a choice. If your phone sends you a school-based email notification, *that* is an intrusion.

Even if you choose not to check email on your phone—which you shouldn't—you shouldn't respond to emails on weekends. Parents and administration do not expect responses outside of office hours, and if you respond and set the precedent once, the unspoken expectation is you will continue to do so. Your time away from the classroom is yours to refresh, to recharge, to take care of yourself and your family.

It can be tempting to check emails over holiday breaks or summer vacation because it can be overwhelming to come back to work after an extended break and already be behind on emails, but checking work email on breaks should be navigated carefully, if at all. Once Pandora's box has been opened, it is difficult to reign back in, and all of the peace you have managed to find during your break from school can be ruined, mutilated beyond recognition by one parent email. It isn't worth the risk.

It is best to check your email and respond to short-task items every morning. If an email will take less than five minutes to respond to, and most will, then tackle those tasks in the morning before the kids come in.

Someone's parents may have emailed to explain something that had happened over the weekend or to say a student is out sick, and those are important details to know. Administration might email saying an assembly time has been moved or an event sprang up that the kids need to attend, and you need to know those important scheduling items, so checking your email each morning is essential. Beyond that, try to not check again until the kids have left at the end of the day.

If you check during your planning period, it can quickly overcome the short amount of time you have to lesson plan and grade papers. If you check during lunch, you are working through lunch, and every teacher deserves to have an uninterrupted lunch period (even if it is only twenty minutes long).

Checking your email again after school will ensure that you have more uninterrupted time on your hands to respond to emails that take a little more time. Some emails are task oriented or "housekeeping" items that don't require much thought or emotion, and whether you answer in the morning or the afternoon, they can be responded to immediately.

Other emails, the ones that make your blood boil and your eye twitch, require a cool-down period of twenty-four hours before you respond. You never want to send off an email that has a negative tone or phrasing that could be interpreted as being aggressive, especially if the response is going to a parent (see the chapter on emailing parents).

Creating healthy routines surrounding email will help to improve your workday and make you a more efficient educator. Constantly checking email can be distracting during the workday, so turn off the volume on your computer, ignore those notifications for new emails, and set boundaries between you and your email.

Fifteen
LESSON PLANNING

Teachers have their favorite content to teach. English teachers absolutely have their favorite set of novels to teach. However, they need to be cognizant of the actual standards being taught. Sure, you have heard this idea before, the idea that you need to know where your kids are expected to be so you can get them there, but this is *real*. Teachers can't just read their favorite novel or do their favorite lesson and hope the standards fall in place. That's not how the educational system works anymore. You need to be able to balance your favorite things with the things you are legally bound to teach.

As fun as debunking teaching philosophies can be, this one actually holds some merit. If you know your kids need to understand characterization, then you need to choose a novel rich in characterization. You can't just choose your favorite novel and hope for the best. Each class has a certain set of standards that need to be taught and if teachers are lucky, they have the opportunity to tackle how those standards are going to go down.

If you are one of those lucky teachers who get to write their own curriculums, this can be a very daunting task. When you get this wonderful opportunity, start at the end. Look at how many skills need to be taught throughout the school year. Then, decide which ones need to come first in order to tackle the next. Once you understand the standards, divide them up by quarters within the year. Each quarter can then be broken down into smaller sections. Notice there hasn't been mention of content yet.

The materials used to teach those skills come last. You might be able to teach your favorite unit still, but you may need to do it at a different time in the year. Doing this front loading will save you so much time throughout the year.

The writing of each lesson plan can take some serious time. But, once you have your standards laid out, the actual writing of the lesson plan can become a faster process. Each administrator might want something different included in the lesson plan but here is what you can use to make the lesson planning more efficient and effective. The chart below could be a living document. If administrators don't require anything more, throw this in a Google document and share it with them and update it weekly or biweekly (depending on what they require in your school).

This isn't so much a lesson plan as it is a blueprint. But, it might be enough to appease the people checking your lessons (table 15.1).

Table 15.1

Standards	Dates	Assignments, activities, and/or assessments	Homework
List the standards in the order you plan on teaching them.	Assign the date range you plan on tackling them.	List the stories you might read, chapters you might cover, ways you might assess the skill, etc.	Any homework for the day

What is good about this living document is it can be easily modified. As most of you know, in this field, your days get absolutely ruined with something completely unpredictable. A kid might pull a fire alarm and because it wasn't scheduled it takes 40 minutes to sort out while you stand outside in the scorching Florida sun (or snow ... or rain). Teachers need to be flexible in their scheduling, and adding date ranges—like Monday 3/2–Friday 3/6 will add some flexibility.

Kids don't really see this document. What you can do for them is simpler. Print a blank calendar page and fill in the plan for the week or day for each month. Really, just outline what content you are covering. This helps if they are absent. If you are reading a short story or conducting an experiment Monday and Tuesday, write that on the calendar. If the unit test is on Thursday, write that down, too, so they can't say they didn't know about that test.

Creating exciting assignments that the kids will enjoy doing is part of the perks of the profession. Teachers want kids to enjoy learning, right? However, the actual planning of the lessons can be difficult and time-consuming so it is worth the time to find something that works for you and your administration.

Sixteen
PHOTOCOPIES

There is never a good time to need to use the copy machine. The best-case scenario is to get yourself a student assistant and have him or her make all the copies you will ever need. Some schools have systems where you only get an allotted number of copies you are allowed to make within a semester. Other schools will do all your copying for you if you get the originals to them a week in advance. At other schools, the copies are like the wild west, hope you get there first and strike gold (a.k.a. the copier has ink, isn't jammed, and there isn't a line).

The transition to online learning and the widespread use of Learning Management Systems, such as Google Classroom, Canvas, and Schoology, have made copying documents less time-consuming, but they haven't fully eliminated the need for physical paper, and the copy machine will still be a beast you need to tame.

Your first job will be to learn how to use it. If you have a mentor teacher in your building or a department head, turn to them first. A principal's secretary might also be willing to give you a quick tutorial if you are in a pinch, but try not to catch them in the morning (because those hard-working individuals are usually SWAMPED in the mornings). Once you learn how to do the basics, jot down the model number so you can dive onto the internet and watch a few YouTube videos walking you through how to use some of the advanced features (this is time well spent. Guaranteed).

Once you know how to use the machine, you need to time your visits properly. At the beginning of the year, everyone is making handouts for open house night, for the first day of school, for syllabus and schedules and expectations and opening day activities. The copies fly fast and furious those first few days before kids come back to school. If you want to get some copier time during these opening days, try to find one in a tucked-away part of the school.

If *that* doesn't work, try to come into work about ten minutes early and go straight for the machine. Beat them all to it and be ready with every original you need a copy of. If *that* doesn't work, you might need to try going right before the end of the workday. Most teachers will have finished with the machines by then and they will usually be open, or at the very least, less crowded. This is also a good strategy for right before midterm or final exam testing when there are bound to be more teachers copying study guides and exams.

The best plan for photocopies is to get ahead and stay ahead. If you are lesson planning for a week at a time (or two weeks ideally), then take all of the originals you think you will need copies of and decide:

- Can projecting this on the board be sufficient?
- Would this be better shared electronically through our Learning Management System?
- If kids need it in hand, will a class set be enough, or will each student need a copy for him or herself?
- Will the kids be working in groups? Perhaps I only need 8 copies of this? Can I put them in sheet protectors?
- Can I put a class set of this in sheet protectors and let kids use dry-erase markers to write on it? For a high school class that could turn 130 copies into 25.
- Could I use dry-erase boards for multiple-choice practice?
- Could I use a Google Form or Kahoot.com for multiple-choice questions?

Once you know how you plan to use each document, write the number of copies you need on a sticky note and place it on the cover of each document. Place all of those originals into a file folder labeled "To Be Copied" and carry it with you everywhere. This way, if you stumble upon a few extra minutes and an unoccupied copier in front of you, you are prepared to crank out a few copies.

Seventeen

KEEPING UP WITH GRADING

Students should be working hard to complete meaningful tasks helping to build them toward subject mastery, and the teacher's role is to focus on providing feedback on how the student is progressing toward their goal of subject mastery.

This can be daunting, so there needs to be ways to make this manageable.

In fact, every part of teaching could be considered daunting . . . and time-consuming. Preparing for lessons: time-consuming. Teaching students: time-consuming—most of the time is actually spent here. Providing feedback for student work: time-consuming and especially daunting because if not managed in a timely manner it just piles and piles higher.

Students need relatively swift feedback on their work in order to know if they are getting the skill correct and should continue practicing the way they are or if they are incorrect and need to make adjustments to their practice. Providing students with specific, helpful, and timely feedback can become challenging if you try to provide meaningful feedback for every single assignment, especially if you teach upper grade levels and have multiple courses with over 120 students.

The grading can quickly pile up and become overwhelming, a herculean task that leaves them questioning whether or not those old assignments can just be practice points. Here are a few tips to battle the grading load:

- *Schedule in some independent working time for the kids.* There is no shame in having them work independently so you can catch up on their assignments.
- *Stagger projects.* Giving students a project that will last them three to five days is a glorious time for teachers to get caught up. However, if all of your courses are all working on projects, that is only three to five days of teacher alone time. Instead, stagger the projects. For English I, as an example, they can work on a project the first week of September, AP Literature gets their project the second week, and Intensive Reading that third week. By staggering, your alone time is extended, and you can get caught up.

- *Also stagger larger writing assignments.* If you have multiple preps, don't give all four classes an essay to write at the same time. That's just madness. Stagger the essays and stagger the due dates.

The notion that work should be graded the same day it gets turned in, or even a two-day turn-around, is ludicrous. Some teachers have over 120 students and it is impossible to grade 120 assignments and have them returned. It just can't happen and that should not be the expectation.

This will be said in other parts of this book, but it needs to be said as many times as it takes for teachers to hear it. Your time is your time. Stop bringing home bags of work to be graded every night. Admittedly, there are times when you are willing to sacrifice your night to get caught up. But, it should be some mindless grading like running through multiple choice or practice planning for essays, or something you can do while watching some trash tv.

If, and when, you fall behind, there are ways to catch up. You can assign those projects discussed earlier, or, and this is a personal favorite, have the students pick which assignment you grade for quality.

If you have a few rounds of essays sitting in the bin, pass them all back and have the students decide which one they want for a quality-check, which one they want for practice points, and which one they hang on to for another assignment, like peer editing. Peer editing is a life saver. The kids actually like when this happens because they feel they have more control over their grade. If they know they bombed an essay, there's an out for them.

Do the same thing for any extended response questions. If you gave them ten questions and all ten required extended responses, have them go back through and highlight their three strongest out of the ten they answered. Those three, grade thoroughly. Those three are the ones you can hold against a rubric. The other seven? Check to make sure they had the right idea.

In a perfect world teachers would be able to keep up on the grading. But, once one stack is graded, four more pop up. It's a cycle. Do your best, find a method that works for you.

Eighteen
BUILD IN WORKDAYS

Falling "behind" can happen quickly as a teacher. One minute you literally are all caught up on grading and then kids turn in a homework assignment, and you are behind again. It happens so fast.

Teaching can become an endless cycle of stubborn to-do lists refusing to get checked off during the school day because you are teaching your students, monitoring their progress, providing small group interventions, and doing all of the things needing to be done so your students can learn. However, you are not a robot. You need time to catch up *during* your contract hours. Working at home is fine—sometimes. It happens. But it shouldn't be the norm.

If you are currently working countless hours at home—no judgment. Many teachers have been there. But, the goal is to break out of this pattern. The goal is to get some of *your* time back. This doesn't make you a bad teacher.

How can you alleviate working at home? Build in worktime for yourself and your kids during the school day. This isn't usually possible in the first few weeks of school. Those first few weeks, sometimes the first month, your kids require constant feedback and handholding, and positive reinforcement. They need to know you are paying attention, you are fair with your rules, and you have high expectations of behavior and work. Once those are established though, you can release the reins a bit and allow students time to work independently on a task—without you guiding and handholding.

You will be able to steal ten-minute chunks of time where you can stand at a table or sit behind your desk and grade a quick stack of papers, or read and comment on a couple of essays.

Then you need to take a lap. Ensure students are working, ensure they don't have any questions, and continue your workday. If your students are all engaged and on task, you might be able to stretch your laps out to every fifteen minutes, but you will still need to get up and make sure kids aren't sneaking a cell phone into the mix or getting distracted by a peer. You might want to put some easy-to-grade assignments on a clipboard and check them as you circulate the room.

Giving your students time to work independently builds soft skills they will need to develop such as time management, elimination of distractions, problem-solving, and application of skills previously taught. Providing students and yourself worktime does not make you a bad teacher. It makes you a practical one.

Ways to keep students engaged while providing meaningful work time could include:

- Reviewing a test and making revisions on what they got wrong (using the textbook as a resource, not you)
- Reading a book and annotating for a specific literary element such as imagery or personification
- Writing a response to an article from the previous day
- Filling in a study guide for an upcoming test or exam
- Answering questions about a YouTube video using Edpuzzle or a similar website (make sure they have headphones)

The goal is for students to be actively engaged in what they are doing and to ensure the task is meaningful and within their academic reach. If the task is too challenging, they will have too many questions and the day will backfire—you won't get anything accomplished because they will have endless questions.

Workdays could occur every two weeks, or once every week in a half for secondary. For elementary, a whole day is most likely not going to work, but there can be blocks of time where students work independently, and you can catch up on a little grading. Strategizing to save yourself unpaid working hours is necessary to avoid getting burned out on your hours off. Those hours need to be preserved as much as possible, and workdays can help to accomplish this.

Nineteen

THE TEACHER BAG

Do you carry entirely too many bags to work each day? Are you weighed down by a purse, a lunch box, a briefcase, a teacher bag? Are you lopsided from carrying daily lesson plans and materials to be reviewed and papers to be graded? It is surprising more teachers don't look like Quasimodo by now. Does anyone give trophies for how many bags a teacher carries each day?

If you were to think about your teacher bag realistically, how often does it never leave the car? Or how often does it make it into the house, only to be ignored and brought back to school the next day? Most teachers are utterly exhausted after a day of teaching, so it is no wonder these bags of tasks are not a priority, leaving all the pens and highlighters hibernating in the bottom of the bag for just one more night.

On the weekends, when, conceivably, teachers are a bit fresher, they need to do all the things that didn't get done during the week. They need to grocery shop and clean the house and go to their kid's soccer games and do yard work and catch up on laundry. The list is endless. Where is the teacher bag in those moments? Home? In the trunk next to the milk and eggs and cleats?

If you are feeling plagued by the presence of the teacher bag, allowing guilt to wrap itself around you on Sunday evenings as you trudge out to the car instead of curling up on the couch to watch mindless television, leave the bag in the trunk. Better yet, leave it at school.

Break the cycle.

If you can't, if that bag is your lifeline to your classroom and to your kids, then fine. Bring it home. But refuse to allow it to ruin your time with your family or infringe on your sanity.

If you like your teacher bag, try to weed out what comes home from your classroom. If you find lesson planning fun, then bring that home. Professional development books can come home (because you *certainly* don't have time to read most of those during the school day, except this one, of course). Big stacks of grading can come home . . . sometimes, near the end of the grading period. The goal is to limit what gets into the teacher bag and leave out anything that will cause stress or angst. That nonsense can stay at school where it belongs.

The teacher bag is a powerful tool if wielded properly. It has the ability to make you feel organized, in control, and productive, which is important. But at home, we don't need to be any of those things if we choose not to be. On weekends, if you insist on bringing the bag home, leave it in the car and relax. Or, if you are able, leave that sucker at school. Schedule your time differently while you are in school and use *that* time to be the super-teacher that you want to be (table 19.1).

Table 19.1

Safe to bring home	Leave it at school
• Professional development books • Lesson plans for a fun activity • Grading that is easy • Lesson plans that you need for the next day (not the rest of the week)	• Big projects that need to be graded • Lesson planning for an observation • Anything dealing with parent communication • Grading that makes you frustrated/sad • Anything that requires more than ONE bag
Tips for Saving Time Grading (explored more fully in other chapters)	
• Allow students to complete some assignments that AREN'T graded for quality. • Give students independent work time where YOU get a chance to get some grading done. • Lock your door during your planning period, and GRADE! • Allow students to peer-score during practice exercises.	

Twenty
LEAVING FOR THE DAY

When the bell rings signaling kids can leave for the day, collective sighs can be heard across the school as teachers are kid-free for the first time in hours.

It can be tempting to dive onto social media to see what you have missed in the world for the last eight hours, but making social media part of your routine at the end of the day, regardless of how satisfying it is, isn't the best use of your time.

The routine you follow before you leave your classroom for the day should work to bring the day you just completed to a satisfactory close and to make the next day easier.

You can do this by:

- Organizing the assignments students turned in throughout the day. Use paper clips and binder clips, sticky notes, and trays. Organize them in whatever way makes sense to you. Then decide which assignments need immediate grading and which can wait until tomorrow. If you have time at the end of your day, within contract hours, grade the assignments requiring timely feedback. Try not to bring them home if you can help it.
- Checking your email before you leave for the day, just to make sure you have everything you will need to know for the following day.
- Organizing your lessons for the next day, especially if you need photocopies or other materials ready for the morning. Getting all of this gathered before you leave for the day helps to ensure the following morning runs smoothly (or, at least, smoother) and can free up time in the morning if there are unexpected interruptions to your routine.
- Organizing your desk. Chances are, throughout the day, you ended up with nurse passes and extra copies and stray to-do lists and seventeen pens all over your desk. Tidy up. This serves two purposes: one, it allows you to start the next day with a fresh slate, and two, it creates a tidy space just in case you need to have a substitute the next day.

- Leaving your emergency substitute teacher folder in the middle of your desk. It may sound overdramatic, but you never know what may happen from one minute to the next, especially if you have kids of your own. Teachers are all just one flat tire or stomach flu away from needing a substitute to start the day in our stead, and if your folder with emergency plans is out on your desk, you have one less stressor for you in the event of an emergency. If you don't need it, you can tuck it away as soon as you get to work the next morning.
  - Your emergency plans should include:
    - Student rosters for every class period
    - Seating charts (if applicable)
    - An overall schedule of the day
    - A copy of the class expectations
    - A list of routines the kids are accustomed to following
    - A generic lesson applicable to any time of the year and isn't unit-dependent (unless you plan to update the folder frequently)
    - A list of emergency phone numbers within the school in case the substitute has questions or problems arise

Leaving on a Friday is a little different than leaving on a Tuesday. Before you leave work on a Friday, ensure your room is tidy *beyond* your desk. Have books been placed where they belong on the shelves? Has trash accumulated in any corner of the room? Do you have extra copies from four weeks ago ready to be recycled? A weekly room check-in will help to eliminate the accumulated clutter classrooms naturally produce.

Twenty-One
STAY ORGANIZED AND WRITE EVERYTHING DOWN

Invest in a great planner! Some teachers can probably navigate solely on digital planners but not everyone can live their lives that way. Paper planners are where it's at for many teachers. And, it takes days and several stores to find one that will meet all the needs of a very busy teacher. It's worth the investment. It would be impossible to count all the times being fired would be an actual possibility without a planner because so many meetings, important deadlines, before and after school duties, would not have been remembered.

Find an amazing planner and carry it around with you. Always. Make sure it has lined paper in either the front or back for meeting notes and carry it around with you like it's your oxygen tank. Not being able to keep track of dates is not a sign of weakness. No one will judge you if you take a minute to write down important information.

Teachers have so much to balance and remember that it is impossible to keep track of all the balls being juggled in the air, with chainsaws, and delicate china . . . over an alligator pit. You never know when your administrator will randomly ask if you have a random Tuesday at 7 a.m. free for a meeting. Impromptu meetings happen. Don't be that person who immediately agrees and then has to reschedule because of a scheduling conflict.

Also, use your planner for daily to-do lists. There are planners that you can completely personalize and some have a space for meetings, due dates, and a daily to-do list. Some even have an after-school section because some teachers have a problem saying no to things (there's a chapter for that, too).

Once you write down your due dates, meeting times, to-do lists, and after school obligations, highlight it or cross it out once it's finished. Your planner will be colorful chaos but it is so satisfying at the end of the day, or even the week, to see the planner completely highlighted. Plus, when your spouse makes fun of you for trying to go to sleep at 7 p.m., you can open your planner and point. No words are necessary.

If a planner isn't the right route for you, you need to figure out what is. The more you get involved within the school, the more responsibilities you have. There are meetings, and deadlines, and all other time-sensitive priorities that must happen and it would be irresponsible and unprofessional to miss them. Perhaps a dry-erase calendar you hang on the wall would do it for you? You could bring sticky notes with you to meetings and write down what needs to happen on sticky notes with the dates they need to happen and then stick them to the dry-erase board.

The issue with some schools is the unbearable humidity. Once the air gets turned off at night, posters melt right off the walls. Sticky notes don't stand a chance. You'll come in most mornings to a poster crime scene. (On a side note, using a hot glue gun to hold these bad boys up has worked wonders and does not damage the walls as much as other sticky applications.) So, the sticky note idea might only work for some locations.

You have to find something that works for you. This is a hard part of adulting, keeping track of all the tasks and commitments you have to do during and after school. Get yourself a planner and use it. All the time.

Section 4

ESTABLISHING STUDENT ROUTINES

Twenty-Two
COLLECTING STUDENT WORK

One of the worst admissions to be forced to make to a student, parent, or administrator, is the loss of a student's work. This is rarely a confidence-boosting circumstance, and it damages trust between the teacher and the student/family affected. Instituting an organized, consistent, and student-driven system for collecting work almost entirely eliminates this situation.

Learning, when done well, can look a little chaotic, so having an organized place for students to turn in their work can bring order to the chaos. Providing students stacking trays, one per class period for secondary, or per subject area for elementary, allows students peace of mind when they turn work in. Placing a stack of assignments in a random pile on the teacher's desk doesn't feel as "official" as turning the work into a designated space.

When students turn work into the same place, it helps to create routines they can understand and follow. This also helps students from turning work in on random bookshelves or under a pile of folders (which happens). Consistently asking students to turn their work into the same space for every assignment builds an organized classroom where papers never get lost.

Once you have established a consistent system for storing turned in work, having students turn in the work themselves as often as possible is a strategic way to have students take ownership of the turn-in process. If students need to get up out of their seats, walk to the front of the room, pull open a drawer, and place their paper inside of it, there is no way they will "forget" as all their peers perform the same act. They cannot blame a classmate for not turning it in for them. They cannot blame you for losing it. It gives them ownership over the process, thus taking the onus off you.

Student collection mechanisms can be as complex or as simple as you prefer. You could have one large bin at the front of the room dedicated to each class period. You could have stacking drawers labeled for each class period. You could have stacking trays. You could have cardboard mailboxes. You could have designated files in a file box—the options are as open as your imagination as long as the system is logical, fast, and efficient.

Beyond organization, here are some other tips for collecting student work:

- Collect homework at the beginning of the period. Have students place the work in the bin, and then, once they have all had the chance to turn it in, go staple the stack together. This means any student who tries to slip their work in after the deadline will not be part of the stapled stack, and you will know it was late. (See the chapter titled "Establish Routines and Stick With Them" for more on this.)
- Try not to take the grading home. If the grading never leaves the classroom, it cannot get lost in the car, or left on a bus, or accidentally eaten by a dog (all stories I have personally heard from teachers). Other work can come home, like lesson planning. Try your hardest to keep student work in the room.
- For big assignments, like essays and projects, consider having a date-stamper set for the date it is due and stamp the paper or project as it is turned in. If it is missing the stamp and a student tries to turn it in late swearing it was on time, you will have proof it was not, indeed, turned in on time.

It is important to reassure students you do not lose work. This is a common excuse students use when they are *convinced* they turned in an assignment (usually misremembering what they actually *did* turn in or not realizing it is still in their backpack). This is also something students will tell their parents as an excuse for a missing grade in the gradebook. Having routines, structures, and consistency with collecting and grading assignments will reassure both the students, parents, and administrators student work was not lost and proper care was taken on your part.

Twenty-Three
HANDING BACK STUDENT WORK

Students need to know how to store their graded work. All classes are different. Some teachers want binders and tabs and expect all the work to be in there for sporadic notebook checks. Other teachers don't have a policy like this. Some only make them keep their reference handouts and essays. For those teachers, everything else can live at home or be recycled at the end of the grading term. But, it's important students know your expectations and are reminded every time you pass back work.

It's hard for their developing minds to remember your graded work policies because in middle and high school, many of them have possibly six other classes. It doesn't take much to remind them of your expectations when passing back work.

Some teachers rarely hand back work. They hand back assignments that have meaning, like tests, essays, etc., right when they get graded, but classwork that is simply completed for practice lives in this outgoing bin they keep for each class period for weeks. When it does come time to pass back this monstrosity of a stack of graded work, it can take some time.

Here's how you can save as much time as possible while handing back student work:

- List the assignments on the board by color. Red means it needs to go into their folder and green means it's good to go home. This way, when the work does get passed back, they know where it needs to live.
- Leave stacks on desks. When students walk in, they see a stack and know they have been tapped to start passing back the work. Leave about thirteen to fifteen stacks on random desks and try not to pick the same desk too often. Having thirteen kids walk around passing back work is a little disruptive but it cuts the time down significantly.
- Obviously, the more often you do this, the less time it takes because the stack is smaller and the sooner kids get that feedback. Sometimes you might be on top of it and other times you might not. Oh well. Cut yourself some slack.

Work that belongs to students who are absent goes back into the outgoing bin. You should store that graded work until the student returns. You might need a bin for every class period to make the passing back process easier—you don't want to have to sort before passing back work. Using those white Tupperware ones with drawers can make this affordable and convenient. When the drawer or tray is full, pass back work. There's no way you can effectively work with stacks of graded work living carelessly around you. Get them tucked away and out of sight until you find the right time to pass them back.

Assignments that were only practice points should be the only assignments that go into those outgoing graded-work bins. Those assignments can be passed back at a more convenient time later. The assignments graded for quality should go back to students right away. Here's why—if you take the time to grade something for quality, the students should take time to look it over and reflect on their learning.

Be sure to remind students what they need to do with your graded work and where they need to store it. Handing back student work is an underrated duty. It has to happen—quite often, actually—yet no one really teaches you how to do it and it can take quite a chunk of time to figure out how to get it right. Find a method that works best for you. It might take several school years to perfect this task, and that's OK.

Twenty-Four
ASSIGNING WORK

People like routines. Especially kids. Consistency is key to a well-functioning classroom. Isn't this why we spend so much time at the beginning of the year establishing routines? Normally, bucking against the weight of typical cliche classroom management techniques would be here, but this cliche holds up. Routines matter.

When assigning work, these routines matter greatly. If the way you assign work is inconsistent, students have no idea what's going on and what you expect. If some days you have them on Google Classroom, but other days on Canvas and then some days using paper and pencil they will get confused and then teachers get frustrated when students don't know what's going on and then students get frustrated when teachers get frustrated. It's not a slippery slope fallacy when it's true, right?

When students walk into a classroom, they need to know what to expect. For example, they could see a slide presented on the board with their bell ringer. What they could also see is a timer. Have the same slide every day when they walk in. Don't change the format and don't change the type of bell ringer. They could also answer that bell ringer question in the same notebook every day. This routine should rarely change. When the timer is up, move on and they can put their bell ringers away. Easy.

At the bottom of the slide, instruct them to write down their homework. Homework can be a confusing component of assigning work, and expectations can definitely get muddled, misconstrued, or forgotten. If homework is inconsistent, students will most definitely forget to do it. Even with college level high school courses, they need a reminder to write it down. Even if they just need to study for a test or read a few pages, have them write it down in the same spot every day, and remind them about it. The routine will be consistent even when assignments will be different.

For any general-level classes, homework needs to be consistent too. Even if you don't give them homework and they need to finish the classwork from that day if they run out of time, there needs to be a predictable routine kids can expect. Have kids circle the assignment title in orange highlighter if they need to take it home. This routine will remind them of the expectation to finish the work and it will remind you which students needed more time. Whatever routine you choose, be consistent in reminding them their work now needs to be completed on their own time.

Dedicate a section on the board for homework, and update it daily. Remind them to check the board when they come in, remind them about the work before they leave, and, most importantly, remind them to turn it in the next day on the same slide that houses their bell ringer.

If the students never have homework, and then all of a sudden, halfway through the school year, the teacher throws them some homework, they might protest, or forget to do it, or refuse to do it; it is out of the ordinary and most kids don't like change. If you know at some point you will want them to have homework, train them with really small assignments a few times a week. Have them complete one math problem a night or watch and take notes on some science-related video online. It will take under five minutes, but they will become comfortable with working at home.

Also, something learned the hard way, when assigning larger projects, it works best to divide that project into steps. Once you have the steps, assign days to those steps. For example, by the end of class on Monday, students should have completed steps 1–3. This works wonders for upper-level kids and is a complete game changer for remedial or on-level students. Kids haven't mastered time management yet. Teachers must help them learn how to do this.

Also, and this ties into the chapter about keeping up with grades, if you can, walk around and check steps 1–3 once they are supposed to be complete, breaking down the larger project into smaller sections to grade will save you so much time!

Overwhelming amounts of frustration can be avoided with clear expectations. If students know where to find the assignments, how to do the assignments, and how to turn in the assignments, they are more likely to do those assignments.

Twenty-Five

BEHAVIORS REQUIRING ROUTINES

Humans are creatures of habit. Think of your local grocery store. When you go in, what direction do you head first? Where do you go next? What is the final stop on your shopping journey? Can you picture it? Assuming the answer is yes, why might this occur? Why can this behavior be predicted? Because most people crave routines and structures; they help us leave our brain space available for higher-order thinking. What happens when the grocery store rearranges? Chaos ensues.

Students feel the same exact way in the spaces they visit every day. They may not be shopping for lettuce in the cooler against the far-right wall, but they are looking for the extra pencils. They are searching for the trash can. They want to know where to turn in their paper or where to find a tissue (and hopefully hand sanitizer).

In previous chapters, there have been many routines mentioned, but honestly, that is because they are so important to a smoothly functioning classroom environment. Many secondary teachers forget what elementary teachers know for certain: without routines, a class can fall into anarchy. While secondary teachers may not need to walk their students to and from lunch or to specials, students, whether eight or eighteen, still need to know what behaviors and routines to expect in each of their classes. Classes are filled to the brim with students whose behaviors need to be managed so learning can occur.

The following tasks require routines students are familiar with and perform consistently:

- Locating the essential question/standards on the board
- Looking at/copying down the homework and other important information
- Sharpening pencils (but not while you are instructing)
- Throwing away trash (NOT NBA style)
- Asking to use the restroom
- Requesting permission to use the library/go to the nurse
- Turning in assignments (heading papers, where to find staplers, how you want them in the bin/tray, where the tray is located? Which tray/bin their work belongs in)

- Distributing materials
- Finding materials in the room (pencils, crayons, spare paper, scissors, glue sticks, etc.)
- Sorting and storing materials when they finish with them
- Asking a content-related question
- Changing room locations (like going to an auditorium or the library)
- Understanding fire drills/ tornado drills/ other emergency drills
- Using cell phones (see the chapter titled "Battling Cell Phones")

Routines work best when they are: introduced naturally as the need arises and if the expectation is explained before the action, explained clearly, performed with supervision, and praised when executed properly. It only takes a few times of performing the task for the routine to stick, and the desired behaviors will eventually occur without your supervision, but in the beginning, as you try to develop these routines, it is essential you supervise and provide feedback.

A checklist on the board at the end of a project or particularly messy assignment will help kids to remember multiple procedures that need to be accomplished. A checklist could also be on cardstock folded like a table tent right on the table the students are working on, then you can require them to initial after each step or task has been completed.

It is also helpful if routines begin right away, early in the year. These routines shouldn't be taught in isolation—kids don't need to be parading around the room practicing taking out and putting away scissors without ever cutting a piece of paper—but kids need to learn to navigate the room in small doses, a little at a time, learning routines as they engage in content. Choose content-driven activities early in the year that require routines and teach the routine simultaneously. Students can develop bad habits quickly, so the sooner routines are authentically established, the better.

Section 5

DEALING WITH ADMINISTRATION

Twenty-Six
DON'T PANIC WHEN THEY CALL (OR EMAIL)

Let's be real, it is always a little unsettling when an administrator calls your room or emails you asking you to come to see them during your planning or after school, *especially* if they don't put any context in the request. A vague call or email can send even a veteran teacher into a bit of a tailspin wondering, "What did I say?" or "What did I do?" or "What did I forget to do?".

Most likely, the reason you are being called in isn't too horrific. If it was bad (fireable or formal reprimand-level bad), there would be clues:

- There would be an official time to go down to see administration, not just a "stop by." (Disclaimer: A specific time in the request does not predicate you automatically being in trouble; your administrator might just be incredibly busy and doesn't want to keep you waiting.)
- They interrupt your class to pull you out. Finding coverage for teachers can be challenging, especially with a short turnaround time, so if an administrator arranges coverage for you and asks you to go down to his or her office immediately, this might be a moment to feel a little trepidation. It doesn't automatically mean you are in trouble, but something time-sensitive might be happening.
- If you are in a union state, you might be asked to bring union representation with you to a meeting. If this is the case, listen. Bring the union representation, because whatever happens in that meeting, you will want backup. The same is true if you walk into a meeting and there are two or more administrators in the room. If the conversation starts to turn in a direction where you think you might have made a mistake, bring in your union representative.

Beyond those three rather increasingly extreme scenarios though, it is unlikely you have any cause to panic. If these haven't occurred, your admin could be wanting to discuss ANY number of topics necessary to run a balanced, orderly school. These topics might include:

- A friendly check-in (especially if you are a new teacher or new to that school)
- A parent question/concern (if you teach secondary, chances are it is regarding a grade, not you personally)
- A question about content (are you reading an edgy book with your kiddos? Watching a hot-topic documentary? If you are, GREAT! I bet the kids are engaged and learning. Don't sweat—as long as it connects to your standards and you can articulate the curricular connection, you are fine).
- Teaching assignments/preferences for the following school year
- Sponsoring a club (administrators *know* it is harder to say "no" face to face rather than through an email)

There are *so* many reasons an administrator may ask you to visit his or her office. They don't all require you to turn into a giant tangle of anxiety. A little anxiety is normal, but don't let it consume your whole day.

If you find yourself hyper-focused and diving into an awful mind space of playing "worst-case scenario" with yourself, try focusing your energies on this checklist quickly (less than five minutes of time), and then MOVE ON with your day:

- Consider the last forty-eight hours in your classroom: did you write any referrals or have any interactions with students or parents requiring follow-up?
- Did any big-point assignments just get put into the gradebook? If a kid drops a letter grade or two overnight, there might be a potential cause for alarm for many parents.
- Consider the content you are teaching. Does it align with grade-level standards?

After quickly running through this list, take a deep breath. Relax. Don't dwell on these. These are normal concerns brought to administrators and shouldn't result in much more than engaging in a follow-up conversation. The point to remember here is to relax. Focus on the tasks and students in front of you until it is time to head to the office, and after the meeting, as you leave the office knowing everything will be okay, smile, push back your shoulders, and reassure yourself you are doing a great job.

Twenty-Seven
INFORMAL WALK-THROUGHS

Don't panic. It never fails that administration walks in when someone is acting a fool, the class isn't super engaged in the lesson, and/or you finally take a moment to sit down. But, not every day can be a dog and pony show, right? Exactly. That is *exactly* why administration does these walk-throughs. When teachers schedule their formal evaluations, it takes quite some time to prepare for those, right? Who has time to do all that prep for every single class period every single day? No one. More importantly, who has that kind of energy? Well, a brand-new teacher might, but shouldn't be expected to.

Don't blame the administration team for these walk-throughs. What they look for is important, and they are questioned when students don't perform well. Think of it more like they're covering their own butts and less like they don't trust you to do your job. Don't think they are coming in for "gotchas." They come in. They document that learning is happening. Period. This is what you might need to remind yourself every time.

They aren't here to catch you off your guard. They are here to document cool things are happening and even if your students don't perform like you want them to, learning is happening. Because it is. Kids are learning.

Every day.

Every school is different. But, most administrators look for most of the following:

- Kids on task
- Kids engaged
- Objectives displayed
- Lessons match objectives
- Students know the goal of the lesson
- You're not at your desk napping

If students happen to be on the independent portion of the lesson when an administrator walks in, casually remind them of how they are being assessed, what the end goal is. A quick "hey guys, remember the goal is to show me you know how to incorporate textual evidence in your responses so be sure to hit that mark." A quick cue will keep students on task and cue administrators on what they are seeing.

If administration walks in and you're in the middle of lecturing, don't forget to throw in these little strategies: call on students, prompt them if they don't have the correct answer, and give them some time to think if they need a minute. You can also call on students to answer questions about past assignments that feed into this current task. Ask them about what they did yesterday to help prepare for what you expect them to do now. If you don't trust your kids to do this, do it yourself. Remind them what was done yesterday and explain how that feeds into the lesson of the day. Reflecting on past learning experiences is a golden ticket.

Be sure to walk around. You really should be doing this anyway. Assigning a task and plopping down at your desk is not good teaching practice. But, what if this was your day to catch up on grading? Well, damn, because now you have an audience. If they catch you at your desk, start calling up students to conference about their grades. This way, it seems natural that you are at your desk and there is a good purpose for it.

Make it a habit to conference with students individually about their grades anyway throughout the year so students know where they stand and what they need to do to improve (and, so they don't make it weird when you do this during a walk-though).

If students have a workday, like a makeup day for all their missing work, make sure you state that on the board. Maybe even include a timer. If an administrator walks in and some kids are working on old assignments, great. However, some kids do everything that is expected and might be playing on their phones. You can be good with that. They worked hard and deserve a break and that break can easily be defended to any administrator. On the board, next to the agenda for the kids making up work, state that if students have everything turned in they can spend the period how they want.

If you practice doing these things on a daily basis, you can eliminate some stress when they come in.

Twenty-Eight
FORMAL EVALUATIONS

Most teachers have to go through an evaluation process every year, and while this process can vary from state to state and even district to district, most evaluation processes include an observation of your teaching.

Teacher observations are a chance to show your administration what your class looks like on your best teaching day. This is your chance to be yourself with your kids and to show administration the climate you have built in your room. It isn't meant to be stuffy. It certainly isn't the time to try something brand new or decide you are going to finally crackdown on normally tolerated behavior (for instance, gum chewing). This is a chance for you and your students to simply invite your administrator, or administrative team, to get a quick snapshot of your teaching style.

As you start to think about your lesson for your observation, it may be helpful to ask for a copy of the rubric you will be measured against. Once you have reviewed the rubric, you should print out your lesson plan and annotate it, ensuring each point on the rubric is present. Label the rubric comments as you find them and fill in gaps accordingly.

Doing this work as you plan will help to ensure you score higher on the evaluation, and also will improve your teaching practices in general. These rubrics are usually created from a series of best practices, so incorporating them in your classroom leading up to your evaluation is only going to make you a better teacher.

If you have a pre- or post-observation meeting with your administrator, show him or her your annotated lesson—let them see your intentional planning. It isn't cheating to strategize. Remember, the goal of observations and evaluations is to help you grow as an educator, so showing them you are learning and growing as you plan can only help you.

Planning a lesson you are comfortable with and that satisfies the demands of the rubric can be both rewarding and time-consuming, but none of the prep work will matter if you don't have the students on board during the observation period.

Here are some tips for ensuring student buy-in during your observation:

- Choose the time of day wisely (if you get to choose). If your kids are tired and grumpy in the mornings (welcome to the world of secondary students), you may want to choose a time later in the morning. Perhaps avoid having your observation right after lunch or at the end of the day, kids can be a bit wild at these times.
- If you teach elementary, you most likely have the same kids all day, but if you are secondary, try to choose a class period with a group of kids who have a good rapport with you. Even if they aren't the quietest class, having them participate and knowing they are invested in your success will make for a great observation (the quiet kids don't always produce the most engaging lessons for observations anyway).
- Promise the kids you will be yourself. Reassure them they should be on their best behaviors, but they can still be themselves. No shows. *That* should be the promise: just the best versions of everyone in the room.
- Give the kids a quick run-down of what to expect. DON'T teach them the exact lesson the day before. It will be obvious.

The evaluation process is important and can help guide your future professional development, so even if the process doesn't turn out perfectly, enjoy the experience, learn from it, and stay positive. Teaching isn't a job you can master in a year, twenty years, or even a lifetime—that is why there is an entire chapter in this book about always being a learner. This profession is a living, breathing beast needing constant tending and has an ever-moving target of proficiency. Stay flexible, keep learning, and strive for your best. Nobody can ask for more.

Section 6

COMMUNICATING WITH STUDENTS, PARENTS, AND ADMINISTRATION

Twenty-Nine
ANSWERING EMAILS

Choosing the time to check your email is important. Choosing a time and making the time are slightly different ideas. Be very careful. If you are an a.m. checker, then you are more than likely going to get bombarded with many unpleasant emails first thing in the morning. Those nasty parent emails you will undoubtedly get no matter how hard you try can completely change your mood for the day.

It isn't necessarily recommended to wait until the end of the day to check either. You might miss an important meeting reminder or rescheduling or something else crucial. What is recommended is to *wait* to answer those emails that will take more thought—the ones that are not time sensitive and need a moment of reflection. Wait until you have the time to properly answer those parent emails because if your mornings are anything like those of many teachers, they are rushed and hectic. That isn't the proper time to respond to a parent. Field your emails. Set aside the ones that need that cool-down period and address the time sensitive ones early on.

Wait twenty-four hours (if your district allows it) to respond to the emails where parents challenge your entire teaching philosophy. The kind of emails where they basically accuse you of not doing your job correctly or good enough. Those need time. The emails where parents demand to know why their student has a 6% and in that same email demand you do something about it. Well, in order to construct a calm and rational response explaining to this mother that her son has a 6% grade and that matches the same amount of time awake in your class, takes finesse. And, when heated, take a breather before drafting that email.

What's even more important than when to respond is *what* to respond. Table 29.1 shows a list of what should and should not be disclosed in an email to parents. Be wary, though, because different districts may have different policies.

Aside from what information should and should not be included in emails, there are ways certain tidbits of information should be phrased.

For example:

- Instead of telling a parent their child does nothing in class, explain how his lack of participation resulted in his grade. Or

- Instead of "dude, check your kid's screen time because he's completely glued to his phone for my entire class period despite my interventions," you could explain that technology seems to be a huge distraction and instruct the parents to check the student's screen time during your class period. They will most likely see their child has a full-time job watching other kids do stupid dances online. Or
- Instead of telling a parent there is nothing left to do to help their child earn a passing grade, explain all the opportunities you offered their child and firmly and convincingly explain that he/she/they passed on all of those opportunities.

Not all interactions with parents will be this hostile. However, it happens. Parents are protective of their children (rightfully so) but there might be a time when you need to step away from a snarky email. Reading one rotten email can ruin your day, but the goal is to not let the response ruin your career.

Table 29.1

Should	Should not
1. Include information about a parent's child's behavior in class. This is fair game and should be included, especially if the parent is curious about the student's grades or behavior.	1. Include other student's names . . . even if they are the cause of any misbehavior or distraction.
2. Include a list of missing work when a parent is interested in what can be done about their grade.	2. List assignments you won't accept any longer.
3. Discuss their grade if parent's ask. Maybe they can't figure out how to log into the online grading platform.	3. Violate student privacy, especially when writing about students' personal information like grades or medical information.
4. Sandwich method—start with something positive about the child—anything. Then mention the issue. End with something else positive—perhaps a posed solution to the problem.	4. Share information that should not be shared publicly. Most emails are public record.
	5. Be too confrontational in an email to a parent about the kid's issues in class. You'll see mama or papa bear come out in full force.

Thirty
CALLING HOME

Calling parents does not usually make the top-ten favorites list when asking a teacher what they love about their job. Sometimes teachers call home with positive reports regarding behavior or academic progress, and that is applaudable behavior many teachers strive for. However, if you have 180 students and four different courses to prepare for, you may not have time for calling home for praise reports as often as you would like. However, when there are behavior or academic concerns disrupting the learning in your classroom, calling home becomes a must.

When there is a problem in the classroom, one of the fastest ways to mitigate the problem can be to call home. Many teachers dread these calls because they can turn into long conversations sometimes sounding more like therapy than problem-solving as parents vent frustrations. Employing the following tips, however, can help lead to professional, quick, and solution-based phone calls home.

Tips for calling parents:

1. Be prepared before you call: Ensure you have the gradebook pulled up, the attendance on screen, and/or behavior tracking document you want to reference.
2. If they do not answer: Leave a brief, professional message stating your name, the name of the student you are calling about (they may have more than one student in school), the class you teach, a general gist of why you are calling (although you should never say what a student's grade is over a voicemail, you CAN say you are calling about a child's grade), and leave a phone number to call you back on—including the extension (NOT your personal phone number).
3. If the parent answers:
    a. Always start with your name, the name of the student, and the course you teach.
    b. Ask who you are speaking with (never assume it is a mother or father).
    c. Say something along the lines of "I am sure you are busy, so I will keep this brief." or ask "Do you have a quick moment to speak with me?" This sets the tone for the quick phone call.
4. Start by briefly describing something nice about the student.

5. Follow up with your concern and describe how this concern affects the child's learning.
6. Close by stating how correcting this behavior can benefit the child both in your class and in life (if applicable). Suggest a potential solution when possible and appropriate.
7. End by thanking the parent for his or her time.

Before ending the conversation, it is best not to leave the parent in a foul mood because when we hang up, we have no idea what the punishment for the child might be. Using the sandwich method and following up a concern with a compliment about the child might help to settle a disgruntled parent.

Another strategy to consider is ending the conversation by offering a specific, actionable solution. This gives the parents the next step to move forward with. If the end of the conversation is on a negative note, then the parent may hang up, may lecture the student, but no genuine change could end up happening. Offering a solution provides an avenue for action.

Keeping the call quick and staying focused on solutions can sometimes be the two easiest parts of a parent phone call. Sometimes those calls do not go as planned, and this is where keeping it professional comes in.

Parents do not always play nice. They may get upset and they may yell. You never need to stay on the phone and be yelled at. Ever. Professionally, in a firm (but not yelling) voice, explain to the yelling parent that he or she will need to reach out to a member of the administrative team to continue this conversation. Then, hang up the phone. Immediately call or email an administrator and explain what happened (they will want a heads up in case the yelling parent calls them). Administrators get paid WAY more than teachers in most districts. Let THEM handle the grumpy parents.

The final advice for calling parents is to keep a log of everything. Every time you dial the phone, write down the date, time, and whether you left a message or spoke with someone. If you spoke with someone, write down their name or relationship to the child and a quick list of what was discussed (keep it brief). If the phone call ended with a parent being upset or yelling, note that as well. Phone logs are for your records in case an administrator ever has questions.

Thirty-One

USING MASS-TEXT ALERT SYSTEMS

Some companies, such as Remind 101 and Class Dojo, allow teachers to text parents and students within an instant, and en masse. This can be incredibly helpful if you need to remind parents about field trip forms or if you want to give an end-of-the-week wrap-up to parents. But this can also be a powerful way to remind secondary-aged students with their own phones about big project deadlines looming or if a date for a test needs to be moved.

There is a bit of a danger to these programs though, and you need to be thoughtful when you use them. People have become quite casual and conversational in texting in recent years, and this tendency cannot translate over to these school-based texting features. Messages should be minimal (you never want to spam a student or family), they should be grammatically correct, and they need to be academically based. Anything you text out to your students or their parents should be able to be seen by every member of your school, the county-level administration, and depending on your state, the newspaper.

In many states, the messages a teacher sends through email or through programs such as these, are public record and can be requested by independent citizens as well as the press. Never send a message you are uncomfortable with becoming a newspaper headline.

This means every message you send should be read and reviewed multiple times to ensure you are sending out your message accurately, with a friendly tone and a definitively academic purpose.

Another word of caution with these platforms—they do not replace phone calls when there is a concern about a student. There are too many scenarios where this could go wrong. You should not use text-based messaging to connect with individual parents about behavior issues or grade concerns. Tone is challenging to interpret through text and a weighty conversation should be talked through, even if it takes longer than a text might. Tips for how to appropriately use texting systems are located in table 31.1.

Once you decide you want to open this line of communication up with both your students and their parents, be ready for them to respond. It may sound obvious. Of course, they will respond. Parent communication is KEY!

Table 31.1

Ways to Use Text Systems	Ways NOT to Use Text Systems
• To send out reminders for standardized testing	• NOT to send out testing scores or grades
• To remind students and parents about upcoming field trips	• NOT as a replacement for signed permission forms for field trips
• To remind parents about awards ceremonies or performances	• NOT to replace printed fliers about award ceremonies or performances
• To help keep parents informed when the class moves on to new skills (ex: we finished multiplication, on to division)	• NOT to replace posting lesson plans for administration or for students who were absent
• To remind students about deadlines for projects or to study for a test	• NOT as a substitute for having deadlines and test dates written on the board and reminders in class (not all kids will have phone access)
• To alert students that a class location has changed for the day	• NOT as a replacement for putting a sign on your classroom door

But when you are cooking dinner, or watching a movie, or finally lying in bed watching TV, parents or students might be texting you. Are you prepared to respond? Should you respond? Most likely not. You are going to want to ensure you suspend messaging on weekends, holidays, and after-school hours close at the end of each school day. To keep a healthy separation between your work life and your home life, limit these messages. Time away from school, while it may contain lesson planning and occasional grading, should not be filled with actual student or parent interaction.

Utilizing messaging apps can help you get information out to students and families faster than ever before, as long as you are careful with your grammar, thoughtful with your messaging, and selective about the times you are willing to engage with parents and students.

Thirty-Two
PARENT CONFERENCES

Not every situation can be solved by a text message or a phone call home. Sometimes, parents need to be called into the school to talk to a team of teachers and administrators (or sometimes, they request the meeting themselves). This is normal.

The number one rule is to NEVER meet with a parent on your own. EVER! You should always have an administrator or guidance counselor present for parent conferences. You need to protect yourself as a professional, and getting into a game of he said/she said regarding a student is never ideal, which is why you should always have another school staff member in on the meeting. The end goal of these meetings is the same as the phone call home: focus on being solution-based in these meetings and keep learning as the focus.

Sometimes conferences do not occur due to behavior concerns or academic concerns, but rather as a pre-scheduled yearly event. This usually occurs for students who have special needs of some kind such as ESE students who require accommodations within the classroom or students on a 504 plan where medical concerns necessitate them having accommodations within the classroom.

In these meetings, a member of the ESE staff, the guidance counselors, and the teacher(s) will sit with the parents and student to discuss academic goals and strategies to get the student to reach those goals. The end result of these meetings is usually an updated IEP (Individualized Educational Plan).

Regardless of which meeting type you have been invited to attend, there are a few basic steps to take to prepare for parent meetings:

1. Print up the student's gradebook report and highlight any zeros or failing grades in one color. Highlight any Ds in a separate color. These are areas the parents might be curious about.
2. If the student has the ability to make up any of these low or missing grades, have those copies ready or be prepared to explain when the student can come to make those up. Have a plan in place before you walk in. Be prepared to change it, but being accommodating is a great way to endear the parents to your side.

3. Have a focused list of what you would like to discuss. Limit it to three items (any more feels like a bit of a rant). Having focused talking points will help speed the conference along and will prevent you from drawing a blank if you are asked an open-ended question such as "How has he been doing in your class?". If the parent asks a pointed question you haven't already prepared for, then by all means answer the question, but otherwise, try to focus on no more than three big rocks.
4. Bring a behavior tracking document with you if you have one on this student, especially if student behavior is inhibiting learning.
5. Bring a sample of their students' work (especially in middle and high school where much of the work students do in class rarely makes it home for the parents to see).
6. Bring a copy of relevant testing scores, especially if they are from recent progress monitoring. Beyond grades, parents want to see their child is learning and showing growth, and progress monitoring or state data can demonstrate this.
7. Be prepared to speak to what the student is doing well. Beginning and ending a conference with the positive is a way to leave the parents feeling comfortable and welcomed rather than attacked during a meeting. This is usually called the sandwich method where the "meat" of the conference is sandwiched between two complementary statements.

Even if you are fully prepared with every piece of information, you are keeping the conversation on track, you are being professional and solution-based, some parent conferences go awry. They don't all feel good. They don't all end well. Sometimes parents yell. Sometimes they cry. Sometimes the students cry. There can be a LOT of emotions happening in a parent conference.

Just remember, you do not need to stay and be yelled at in your place of work. If a parent begins yelling at you or calling names, the meeting ends right then. If your administrator doesn't end the meeting, you can politely excuse yourself. Thank them for their time, and leave. Period.

Hopefully, these more emotional parent conferences are the rarity and not the norm, but coming into each meeting prepared and with a positive attitude is going to help foster an environment where a positive parent conference is certainly possible.

Section 7

OPTIMIZING INTERPERSONAL SKILLS

Thirty-Three

TREAT YOUR STUDENTS LIKE RATIONAL HUMANS

Relationship building can be one of the hardest soft skills a teacher builds because there is such a fine line between the strict, no-nonsense teacher everyone loves and will work hard for and the absolute troll who makes students feel stifled with their harsh rules and inflexibility. Teachers who swing the pendulum too far in the other direction end up building fantastic relationships with students, but can lack the classroom management skills and rigor necessary for students to learn.

The goals of any lesson should always be learning and student growth, but just as important is the relationship building that happens when you treat your students like rational human beings and let them see you as one as well.

Teachers are incredibly human and they make incredibly human mistakes. Adults make them consistently and have had *plenty* of years of experience. If the previous statement is accepted as truth, how can teachers expect children, whether they are seven or seventeen, to exist without making mistakes?

They can't.

Students are going to make mistakes. They are going to have a thought, get excited, and shout out their thought in the middle of a lesson. They are going to think of something and immediately feel the need to tell their neighbor in a whisper during silent reading. They are going to forget their homework, think you will be mad, and then perhaps lie about the missing homework. They will lose books, break pencils, need to use the bathroom in inopportune moments, and essentially, be erringly human.

Your job is to teach them not just skills and standards, but to emphasize to them how even in their most human moments, they matter, they have value, and making mistakes and learning from them is one of the benefits of the human experience. We can avoid yelling. We can avoid blaming. We can practice forgiveness and extend grace to students when they make a mistake. Not every breach of procedure needs disciplinary action. A gentle reminder can work just as well.

When teachers turn minor blips of protocol into giant discipline issues or belittle students for their foibles, they lose the ability to build relationships with them, and then learning diminishes.

Relationship building does so much for us in the classroom. When students are on your side, they will work for you. When they know you are fair and consistent and create an environment where students have the ability to learn and still make mistakes, discipline becomes a nonissue (well. Relatively speaking—kids *are* still kids). When students feel targeted, unliked, or unwelcome (whether intended or not) learning has ended.

Treating students like the rational beings they are allows teachers to use small moments as teachable moments in non-degrading or humiliating ways. Try standing next to an off-task student to bring their attention back to where it needs to be. You can keep talking to the class and just walk over and stand next to a student who was talking, and with a simple gesture or reminder, the behavior usually stops. Nobody was embarrassed, nobody got a referral, nobody had to call home, the behavior just stops.

Quietly asking a student to stay after class for a quick chat can be effective, too. If whispering is too obvious, write your request on a sticky note with a smiley face and then place it on the student's desk as you circulate the room. After class, rather than tell the student what they did wrong, ask if they are okay. Ask if the content is challenging them. Ask if there is something troubling them. Ask something that opens the line of communication.

Kids have whole lives beyond the classroom, human lives filled with human concerns, and letting students know we are here to listen can help build relationships far more effectively than chastisement and discipline.

Thirty-Four
KEEP THE RULES SIMPLE

Have the kids make their own rules . . . they said . . . it will get them to buy in more . . . they said. Lies. These are lies. And, the students probably won't include a no cellphone policy. Shocking.

Admittedly, by having kids make the rules, at least they are privy to them. But, has anyone actually seen a student clean up after himself because in week one he said he would? These are not wedding vows, and kids can't remember all the different rules for all the different teachers. Honestly, even remembering all the rules laid out by different administrators is hard to keep track of. Brains are busy during the school day.

As you create the rules for your room, keep them minimal and easy to remember. Trying to make students remember fifteen class rules is ridiculous. It's important to remember that procedures don't have to be rules. If behaviors can be taught, focus on what should be an actual rule. If you can, try to stick to one rule.

This one rule can get the job done, and it is broad enough to cover multiple offenses, yet narrow enough that it is not easily misinterpreted.

> Rule one: Be a respectful human.

Done.

This includes respecting your space, your time, other people's space and time and beliefs. This expectation extends to substitutes too. This includes cell phones while you're actively instructing them. It would be rude to check it when you're talking to them but only mildly annoying when they check it during individual work time. Leaving trash around is disrespectful to your space. Spitting gum on the floor is also disrespectful. Drawing on the desk? Yep, that too. It's easy and the kids can remember it.

Students respect this one rule. Sometimes, toward the end of the year, they forget and start to creep closer to the door, as an example, even though it was explained that packing up early is disrespectful of the time you have with them. But, just remind them that their rush to leave your room hurts your feelings and violates the ONE rule you have, and they will reconsider. The kids might be deviant but rarely are they malicious.

If one rule isn't enough, stick to a low number of rules. If you try to tack on ten class rules then the students will not be able to satisfy you all the time. Rules will be violated because that's a lot to remember, and kids are kids. If a rule is more of a routine, teach it as such (a behavior to be learned and practiced), not told and punished.

Students have rules dictated by their parents, the law, school administration, their social circle, and sometimes six other teachers. They will not remember they can't have gum in your class but can in four others. They either won't remember or may not care to remember. However, the one respect rule means they can't shove their gum under their desk or throw it on the floor. And, they don't. They might actually get up to spit it out when they're finished. If they disrespect your space by dropping snacks, ask them to sweep it up to respect your space. And they will.

Teachers are helping guide their students into adulthood. Regardless of the age you teach, you are preparing your kids to navigate the world around them. Later in life, when your students are grown, they will be in places where detailed rules aren't provided (aside from laws), teaching them to be decent, respectful humans will be a lesson you provided that they carry with them and you may not even know it.

Thirty-Five

CHRONICALLY ABSENT STUDENTS

It is incredibly challenging to teach students who are not present at school. Gathering their work for them can feel like a Herculean task at times, and it feels like even more of a waste when the students don't even complete the missing work. However, there are ways to ensure the missing work gets into the students' hands and that you maintain a relationship with this student even though they may not be in class often.

Attendance issues can sometimes mask home scenarios or personal battles not always articulated in the classroom, so it is always important to keep this in mind when feeling frustrated about student absences. Rather than berate a student or ask them why they weren't in class . . . again . . . tell them you are happy to see them. Let them know you are there to help. Offer to get them their makeup work. Putting them on the spot demanding an explanation for an absence (or string of absences) is not going to make the student want to continue coming to school—especially if they already don't want to be there.

Consider referring the student to the guidance counselor or school social worker if you are under the impression the student needs to talk or might need help, but don't harass him or her when they come into your room. Their emotions most likely are highly taut just being in the room.

Handling the emotions around chronic absenteeism is one battle, but navigating the missing assignments can be a whole other. One of the best ways to handle the missing students' missing assignments is to keep a file folder on your desk with the student's name and every time you hand something out to the class, place the paper in the file folder you created for this student. If you teach elementary school, you hopefully only have one of these.

If you teach secondary students, you most likely have over a hundred students a day, so perhaps have a file folder for each period and write the absent students' names on the tops of their papers and store them in the file for that period until the student returns to collect it.

If you teach secondary, and especially juniors and seniors who can drive, these numbers become a little higher. Perhaps consider a file box with hanging files with the kids' names on them. Just keep them in a place where other students cannot see whose names are listed because singling out a student in a public way for absences could lead to teasing or embarrassment for the student who is chronically absent. The goal is to get him or her to come to class more often, not intimidate them into staying home even more frequently.

If you have students who aren't chronically absent but absenteeism is more of a scattered issue across the class, use a file box with hanging files and number the tabs on the hanging file from 1–31 (one tab for each day of the month).

Then, on the 16th of September, when you pass out an assignment and have five leftover papers, you put those five papers into the number 16 file. Then, if a student was absent on a particular day they know to go to the file labeled with the date they missed and grab their needed assignments. At the end of the month, clean out numbers 1 through 15, and when you fill them again, empty out 16 through 31. This gives students two weeks to make up missing work from absences, which is plenty of time.

Whether you are gathering missing work for one student, five students, or a classroom full of students, it is important to put the onus for grabbing the work on them. At the beginning of the year, show students your system for organizing work they missed. Then, as you notice students return to class from an absence, remind them where to find the work—don't assume they remember. You might need to remind students a few times where the work is before they get in the habit of finding their missing work on their own.

If you try to hand every paper to every kid, it will cut into your instructional time. As much as possible, try to let them handle that themselves.

Absenteeism is never an easy problem to tackle, but with the proper setup and with a proper mindset, it can be manageable.

Thirty-Six
THE LOUD KIDS

Is it believable to say some of your loudest kids might turn out to be your favorites? It's true. After five, fifteen, or twenty years of teaching, how often do you remember the quiet ones? Sure, if prompted, with some reminders, you might remember the quiet boy who sat in the corner and kept to himself. However, the loud ones, the ones you hear far too often and the class is several decibels quieter when they aren't there—those? Those are the ones you remember. Those personalities stick, and often have their own special charm.

Most teachers like their classes to be lively. They don't always discourage talking because if they do it too often, those moments where they do want talking and collaborating, they get nothing. When you want students to contribute to group discussions, but they may have been silenced for too long, the discussions might flop.

However, there is a threshold of noise and discussion that can easily be crossed. A noisy room can inhibit learning, so it is important that these kids don't become a huge disruption and distraction.

These loud kids can be pegged the moment they walk into your classroom. For whatever reason, they want to be seen, heard, and remembered. There are a few ways you can make them feel seen:

- Learn their names quickly and say those names often (not just in a reprimanding way) but more of a "good morning [insert name]."
- If too many students ask you to repeat directions, call on the louder kids to parrot those directions back.
- If you are reading parts of a textbook out loud in class, start with them and let them read until they don't want to anymore and then allow them to call on the next person (but never force a student to read out loud).
- If you need to recap what happened yesterday in class, you might not want to always call on the loud kids because there are other kids who need to practice speaking out in class, but you might ask one of the louder students to list one point the student you called on may have missed or to elaborate on one idea that student said.

- For group work, deliberately pair a less outspoken student with the outspoken one. When putting kids into teams, they usually have roles. The role of the loud one is the ambassador. They are the ones ensuring the other kids are comfortable with their assigned roles and tasks. They will get the supplies, create the group chats, etc. They turn their loudness into leadership qualities.

Now, understand that all students need an opportunity to be heard. Yes. However, when you get into a classroom with struggling or remedial learners then those loud students can most definitely make or break a class. As much as you might want to deny it, they can set the tone. They need to be utilized as an asset and not a burden. They will be loud regardless; you might as well use it to your advantage.

There's a reason they want this kind of attention. They could just be outspoken, confident students. But, those students usually know when it's appropriate to be loud and when it isn't. It's those kids who don't turn the volume off who might have underlying motives. Maybe no one listens at home? It's sadly possible.

These loud kids don't need to be a burden, they can be your greatest assets as long as you create a relationship with them. You may not know their reason for their boisterous personality right away, but the sooner you find out and act accordingly, the better.

Thirty-Seven
THE MEAN KIDS

Kids can be mean, and teachers get the brunt of a lot of frustration. They deflect onto their teachers all that is happening within their lives. Some kids still don't even see teachers as humans. Have you ever encountered a student out in the wild? Like grocery shopping? They look at you like it is so unbelievably impossible you need groceries, too.

For some reason, students see teachers as others. They are not always humans, with emotions, with families, with problems of their own. And, because of this, a lot of their frustration in their own lives manifests into downright rudeness toward any teacher standing in front of them.

The best first step to address a mean student is to speak to them directly and, most importantly, privately. But, this doesn't always work. Sometimes, teachers need to do additional digging to get an idea of where the frustration is coming from and more specifically, why it was directed toward them.

A fifteen-year-old boy once lost his dad unexpectedly at the end of summer vacation. None of his teachers knew this about him. So, it was no surprise that his twenty-four-year-old English teacher had no idea why he was lashing out toward her every single moment of every single class period they spent together. His father was the traditional patriarch, his mother was not typically the decision maker. With the loss of his father, and his mother trying to take on his role, the boy did not respond well. He needed something a female teacher could not provide him and it made him angry. Really angry. He missed that male leadership and mentoring.

In most cases, there are underlying issues. Self-esteem, problems at home, peer problems, etc. Kids are emotional beings, and they are trying to navigate a lot. When girls are nasty to female teachers, it may stem from some low self-esteem. You know what works? Compliment their outfits, shoes, or hair. It takes zero time, and

1. It's hard to be mean to someone when they are actively complimenting you, and
2. It offers them the little self-esteem boost they clearly need.

This works for all students, not just females. Everyone likes to look nice and receive compliments.

Kids aren't only mean to their teachers though, right? Some are just nasty to each other. Schools have implemented the anti-bullying sentiment in full force but even the term "bully" just sounds so childish and many high school students do not take it seriously. Now, teachers report it if they hear about it or see it, obviously, because they are legally bound to. Regardless, if students take it seriously, teachers have to. However, sometimes the meanness doesn't fall under the actual definition of bullying. They are just being nasty to be nasty.

Something that has worked to mitigate meanness and will continue to be used is that the mean kid doesn't get the attention when intervention needs to happen. Instead, try giving it to the recipient of the meanness. If said victim is getting picked on for something they're wearing, for example, gush over how much you like it. Tell them their outfit will be appreciated later by a more mature crowd and they are wise beyond their years or dressed for their future already.

A girl who wore the same pants several days a week due to poverty was saved by this tactic. A girl had said a nasty comment to her. It was only once so it didn't meet the criteria of bullying but still, couldn't be tolerated. It was mentioned by the teacher that her style is the current trend circulating throughout colleges. Students and young adults are buying capsule wardrobes to cut down on consumerism and the movement is taking off. The girl with the pants smiled and nodded as if she was privy to this movement and the other girl said nothing. Nothing more was said about the way she dressed.

Those mean kids need to be addressed. But, this needs to happen tactfully. Teachers don't always know the reason behind the attitude and while it's worth the investigation, that can't always happen on the fly. Perhaps you offended a student early on without even realizing it and that's where the animosity comes from? How horrible would that be? Take the time to get to know those kids and problem solve. They might need you even when they are trying so hard to push you away.

Thirty-Eight
CHOOSE YOUR BATTLES

Your battle cry must be loud. Fierce. But, if you let it rip too often then it loses its power. As much as you want to rip into Johnathan for throwing a paper ball across your room, or for forgetting to put his name on his paper, or dropping the "F" bomb, don't. Not always.

And, the truth is, you can't. You can't because you would drive yourself crazy. Your classroom is your domain and you probably like things the way you like them, but once thirty overgrown heathens walk in for their forty-five-minute sessions, you may quickly realize your domain really isn't yours at all.

Students have power in numbers. Most are too docile to realize this. But the ones who do, the ones who realize who really runs the show—those you need to handle delicately. Sure, you can reprimand David for every cuss word that slips its way into his daily vernacular. But, really, David is seventeen and it just might be a miracle he shows up, stays in his seat, and does his work. You will have to decide which battles you want to tackle with David. You have to decide because as much as you would like to, you might not be able to control everything.

Teachers would make great monarchs. They wouldn't let their pride take over and try to conquer every piece of a territory simply for more control. They would know their limits and they would not be willing to sacrifice just to gain more. Instead, they would conquer the necessary territory: Fertile land, easily defensible, water access, etc. . . . In classroom terms: respect, minimal disruption, hard work. Does it really matter if Jacob balls up his food wrapper and tosses it into the trash can? Not really. It might be disrespectful (there's a chapter for this) but it wouldn't warrant a battle cry because:

1. He didn't stuff the wrapper into the tiny crevices of the desk resulting in ants you have to battle,
2. He didn't take the long way to walk past five of his friends so he could have a hello tour on his way to the trash can, and
3. He did his work quietly while eating his ridiculously small package of muffins.

It will probably depend on your clientele. If you teach teenagers, many can have jobs, drive cars, but might not be able to read well. English class, as an example, might be a damn nightmare for these pumpkins and you can either have allies or enemies.

Some of your students might be old enough to vote, enlist, and yet some teachers might reprimand them for clicking their pens.

Have a battle cry, make it powerful, but use it only when your kingdom is threatened, and your people will listen. A suggestion? Choose no more than four offenses that warrant a battle. Make these known to your kids. They need to know where the line is, but if the line is too long or complicated, they will crush it. It's too much to remember and adhere to. The issue with this: they WILL toe that line. But, rarely do they cross it. There's a chapter about classroom rules, too.

This sentiment works with the higher powers that are within your educational system, too. You can't always be a squeaky wheel because people might tune you out. Be like that cart at the grocery store. Not the one you always seem to grab. It squeals and maybe hugs to the left, and you just deal with it because all wheels at the stores have resistance. Be the one that you know people cannot simply ignore throughout the entire store because the message it screams is loud and clear "something here is broken."

Battle cries should be fierce—and used sparingly. Choose your battles wisely. Make them count.

Section 8

THRIVING AS AN EDUCATOR

Thirty-Nine

CHOOSING YOUR WORK TRIBE

Our schools are full of wolves. They might be four feet tall, missing their front baby teeth and hissing all their "s" sounds, or they may be six feet tall, smelly, and counting down the minutes until they get to drive away in their car and go hang out with their friends, but they are wolves, and they travel in packs. They can sense weakness in their prey and they WILL take their prey down. They will circle, test the waters, and try to catch you when your guard is down. Wolves are clever and ruthless, so you need to be strong. Teachers need people to watch their backs and to hoist them up when they stumble.

Okay, it really isn't that serious, but some days it can absolutely feel that way: us against them, me against the world. Flying solo. Those days are rough. Those days are mentally exhausting and physically draining. This is why it is crucial that you choose our work tribe wisely.

Some teachers will ruminate and joke about the wolves. They see the fangs, they see the claws, but then they go back to their classrooms made of brick, pat the adorable little wolfie heads, and bring them back on track. They focus on the gentle eyes and the soft fur. Make *these* people your people.

Other teachers never stop growling at the wolves. They can't look past the fangs or the claws. They have grown to distrust and dislike the wolves. Stay away from these people.

Teachers should like children, whether they are teaching kindergarteners the building blocks of language or teaching high school seniors AP Calculus, they should enjoy being around kids. The joy of teaching children is that school is designed for them to mess up. Teachers have warning systems and re-do opportunities and grace periods because kids will mess up. School is designed for them to learn more than academic content. Schools are domesticating them, but the wolves aren't there yet. Teachers need to work to surround themselves with teachers who know this, who remember this, and who celebrate the kiddos even when they behave like feral beasts.

Sure, you will all have bad days. You will need to be able to vent to your tribe and find solidarity. You cannot expect the people you choose to be around to be robotically positive all of the time. That isn't realistic (or helpful). But, you need to ensure that after your tribe unleashes all their frustrations in the breakroom, they are the people who go back to the class with a fresh start, a clean attitude, and a gracious heart.

If you surround yourself with toxic personalities, people who focus on faults rather than values, people who can't seem to find a single redeeming quality in his or her students, that is a sure-fire way to bring you down. This toxic person (or group) is not who you want to be associated with. You don't want to be brought down, you want to be lifted up. Attitudes are contagious, and you don't want to catch this germ.

If the goal is job satisfaction, joy and pride in what you do, you need to refocus where you spend your energy. Kids may have claws and fangs, but they have soft souls, and they are moldable. Every child deserves loving teachers, and teachers retain that loving nature by having a tribe who has their backs, and the backs of the kids.

So, if you are a new teacher, choose your tribe wisely. If you are a veteran teacher, think about what kind of tribe you gravitate toward. Regardless of where you are in your journey as educator, you need people because the wolves may be sweet, but they are still wild beasts that need taming. A tribe of one might not survive long without the group to pull them out of the wolf den.

Forty

DECIDING WHERE YOU EAT LUNCH

Finding a work tribe can make lunchtime rather relaxing, even if it is a short little chunk of time. Being able to debrief with co-workers while you eat is a communal bonding experience capable of crossing over grade levels and subject areas. Having a lunch where teachers talk about their hobbies and their families and their weekend plans and their favorite television shows can break up the day and make it more enjoyable.

However, if you find yourself in a lunch group spending their short break eating and criticizing the school's administration, or the School Board, or the students, or the parents, or the curriculum, your lunch can be draining rather than restorative. If you are leaving your lunch period more wound-up than when you entered it, it may be the wrong lunch group for you.

Finding your people, the ones who leave you feeling good about your career, is a special gift. Too many teachers are quick to bash, quick to dismiss, and quick to bring you down.

If you cannot find a lunch group with uplifting people, then perhaps it is time to consider lunch to be a party of one. While eating alone isn't ideal, and having a community at work is important, it is also important to protect your day and your mood and not allow either to be hijacked by negativity. Negativity can be infectious and can change the trajectory of your day, and if taken to heart too many times, the trajectory of your career.

Instead of sitting in a communal lunch space, consider eating outside somewhere else. Perhaps there is a seldom-used picnic table or a bench where you can sit. You might even be able to get to your car and eat while you listen to music. If those options aren't available or ideal, stay at your desk for lunch and play music from your computer. While it is ideal to get out of the classroom, getting into the right frame of mind during your short break is just as important.

If you are too tempted to work while you eat at your desk, clean off a student desk and eat there instead—just be sure to clean it up when you are finished as well. While you are eating, hopefully away from your desk, with music playing from your computer, here are some ways to recharge during this time: work on a sudoku; read a book; do a daily crossword; read a magazine; call a friend; scroll through teacher meme pages on social media (they are hysterical).

Recharging during lunch is important, and finding ways to achieve this while focusing on positivity is essential. Some activities, however, may leave you in a worse mood than when your lunch period started, which will not be fair to you or your students. With this in mind, here are some activities to avoid during your lunch period:

- Any work-related activity you don't want to do (most teachers get an unpaid lunch and nobody should work for free. Lunch is too short for making copies).
- Watching or reading the news: this can all wait until after work.
- Scrolling through social media—a focused dive into social media, like the meme page, is fine. Not too much slander or upset is happening on a teacher meme page. But social media, in general, can be a cesspool of negativity you will want to avoid on your short lunch break.

Preserve the peace of your lunch period. Protect it with the same passion you would protect your morning coffee time. You need a moment to recharge during the day. You need a group of people who will lift you up, not bring you down. If you cannot find them, become them. Invite other like-minded teachers to come and eat with you in your room. Create your own lunch group. Establish the no-bad-vibes rule from day one, and you can have your own social retreat with people who might eventually become your tribe.

Forty-One

KNOW WHAT YOU CAN (AND CANNOT) CONTROL

Teachers like to be masters of their domain, captains of the ship, queens and kings of the castle—when it comes to classroom spaces, the type-A personalities run dominant. Part of this stems from a level of choice and vision rather unique to the teaching field.

Classrooms tend to become an extension of a teacher (since many teachers spend more waking hours in their classroom space than their homes). The freedom to decide how to decorate the bulletin boards, what accessories to put on the desk, what kinds of posters hang on the walls, how books are arranged on shelves—it is all at a teacher's discretion, and that makes *many* teachers *incredibly* happy.

Knowing they can control their preferences for binders over file folders or entrance tickets versus exit tickets (or both) can bring teachers immense pleasure. Even just being able to switch up the colored pens used to grade student work can spark a little kernel of joy. When teaching a standards-based curriculum, many teachers have the freedom to choose what texts and examples they use to teach those set standards, and that level of freedom is what makes most teachers squeal with joy (even if the squeals are purely internal).

There are, however, many, many aspects of teaching where teachers have absolutely no control. None. Zero. Not having control over some of the biggest parts of the job can be absolutely infuriating, but the chart on page 102 offers some suggestions for ways to navigate these issues (table 41.1).

As a teacher, you should not feel powerless in your profession, but you also cannot allow any single one of these to blur your vision or shift the focus from the students who are sitting in your room. These students are unaware of these problems and concerns. They are focused on the teacher in front of them, the books they are learning from, and for the most part, they are blissfully ignorant of the political and bureaucratic concerns crowding public education.

Students attend school to learn, and you are hired to teach them. When investment in these issues gets in the way of teaching, problems arise. Table 41.1 offers ways to feel like we have more control, but those frustrations cannot be all-consuming.

Table 41.1

Potential points of frustration...	But you might be able to...
• Standardized Testing	• Review the test item specifications and find ways to make the test less intimidating for your students
• State-level and national-level funding	• Write letters to congress, to your state board of education, to your governor requesting more/fair funding
• School calendars	• Join the calendar committee for your district
• School infrastructure (building repairs, furniture repairs, etc.)	• Coordinate a group of community volunteers to help with the repairs (with permission from your administration, of course)
• Principal initiatives	• Join the committees leading these initiatives and if a committee doesn't exist, ask your principal if you can help coordinate one
• Teacher certifications/requirements met by the state	• If there is coursework to be completed or tests to be taken, form a study group and make it a group effort
• Teacher duty times	• If they cannot be avoided, try to get duty time with a teacher-friend
• Teaching schedules/courses assigned	• If you have specific preferences, ask the principal early in the year (January or February) for those courses for the following school year
• The adopted curriculum for any given subject	• Supplement the provided curriculum with units you are excited to teach
• The legislation regarding what must (and must not) be taught	• Teach what you must, avoid what you must, but be sure to use whatever autonomy you can to make your lesson plans your own
• The State Standards	• Join the state standards review committees or provide input to the state when they request it
• Medical insurance costs	• Shop around. Many districts won't force you to take their insurance if you already have some of your own
• Teacher salaries	• Join your union bargaining committee

When you find yourself feeling frustrated, look at each face in your room and think of a moment where they had success. Smile at each one of those faces and remind yourself why you went into teaching to begin with—because chances are, it wasn't because you wanted to change the rigor of the state standards. It was because of the kids. Let them be your focus, not the aspects of education you cannot change.

Forty-Two
USING YOUR TIME ON TEACHER WORKDAYS

Teachers are masters at wasting their own time. A teacher's cabinets are never more organized than when there is a mountain of other things that have to happen. Teachers often find friends in their classrooms or the hallways and waste thirty minutes talking about all the things they need to get done. It's ridiculous. But, it's so true. Because there is so much to do all the time, it feels as if there are never blank to-do lists. When the tasks become overwhelming, it is common to temporarily postpone them.

Mastering the art of time management on these workdays needs to become a priority (if it isn't already) because home time is more sacred than school time and avoiding working at home should also be a priority.

To optimize your time on those workdays, begin by making a to-do list of everything that needs to happen that day. Even separate it by class period if you must. You may need to:

1. Grade period one work in the turn-in bin and
2. Grade final exams. Then,
3. Submit grades for period one.

Repeat list for all other class periods. And, that's just your grading to-do list. There may still be a ton of other obligations needed to be met.

Separate those massive tasks into manageable chunks. Grading all 150 exams is a lot and you will never get to highlight the task and check it off your list because it will take you forever to finish (see the chapter about staying organized for information about highlighting).

By breaking down the tasks, you can actually cross tasks off the list. It's a good feeling and propels you forward. Not only should you list all grading, but there is always more to do that is not academic. There's the need to put books away, clean desks, attend meetings, lesson plans, etc. Begin your morning by creating a list. Sometimes, the list has 22 tasks on it but at least you know what needs to go down.

If you really have time management issues, break down those tasks into timelines. From 8 a.m. until 10 a.m., complete tasks 1 through 8. If you meet the goal, get a snack or something. Rewards are always nice. So are snacks.

You also might need to prioritize the list. You might need to reorganize the list so the "must dos" are at the top. You may not *have* to reorganize your cabinets, but you do *have* to get grades submitted. The cabinets would be a nice bonus so it goes to the bottom of the list. Grading at the top. Meetings at the very top.

Something else you can do that is very important is put a sign on your door. There's a meme where a guy has a sign on his shirt telling people not to distract him because he has work to do and he's easily distracted. It's funny because it's true. Interruptions are the perfect excuse to step away from work. Except, don't tell people to leave you alone. That would be rude. Instead, say you'll be available at 11 a.m. or whatever time you finish the tasks that require serious attention—like grading exams.

If you are department chair or program planner, then you might have a lot of teachers who need you. And, as teacher-leaders, you want to assist. However, it will take you twice as long to get through exams if you have constant distractions. By putting a sign up, people will respect your time. After 11 a.m., for example, you can answer a thousand questions while you clean desks, reorganize shelves, put back books, etc. But you can't, and shouldn't, give your kids your divided attention while working on something as significant as grades.

Always tackle the heavy stuff first. If you have mountains of grading, get that done first, do not wait. That stack grows each hour you wait to tackle it. There is a classroom elf who magically makes stacks of papers increase with every passing hour. And, remember, not every assignment needs to be graded for quality (see the chapter on grading for more information).

As much as you might like to shove off that grading, or find your friend and decompress, you have to get work done. You need to maximize your time in order to avoid wasting it.

Forty-Three

DITCH THE RED PEN

Ditch the red pen. Literally and figuratively. Archaic grading technique tells teachers to mark the wrong answers in red. But, what if, and this is a crazy thought, instead, they use a pretty color to mark what was right? Can you put smiley faces or stars on the questions that were correct? How does the mindset of the student change when teachers focus on success rather than failure?

The points stay the same. If you give them a ten-question quiz, for example, and the student got four correct. Instead of writing "-6" on the paper, try writing "+4". The 40% remains the same either way but students automatically see all that was done right and less of what they missed.

Focusing on success matters. Collect an arsenal of colorful pens and be ready to celebrate student success when you grade their work. Give it a try and note the results when students receive their graded work. Pretty colors and stickers don't always have to be reserved for "A"s.

Now, teachers know that students need to learn what was done wrong so they can fix it in the future. Understandable. But student mistakes and shortcomings don't have to be the main course. Treat mistakes like a small side of gross vegetables students have to eat in order to become big and strong. Here's why: consuming too many vitamins and minerals in one sitting just results in the excess coming out in urine. Overdoing the vegetables in one sitting changes nothing. The body does not absorb what it doesn't need. So, by highlighting every mistake, the kids just turn those markings into urine and forget about them.

At the moment, striving learners come to mind. Their egos are already so fragile that they feel they must protect themselves with a thick armor of apathy and attitude. However, see if you notice a difference when you hand them back a paper with pretty teal ink and possibly a sticker, the students might melt just like any elementary school student would because deep down, they need that positive reinforcement—regardless of their age or the grade they earned.

Getting kids to reflect on those assignments graded for quality makes the time spent grading them worth it. That thinking can be powerful, especially when you have them focus on what knowledge was gained.

If you don't want students focusing solely on issues, you can make the process simple by providing a set series of questions they need to answer for each assignment handed back:

1. Explain your effort level on this assignment.
2. Does the effort level match the grade you earned? Explain.
3. Where did you demonstrate new knowledge?
4. Which parts of this assignment makes you the proudest? Explain.
5. Where could you make some improvements? Explain.

By switching this grading mentality, a positive and unexpected side effect is that you might get less angry or disappointed when grading student work. It's disheartening to see that the hard work you put into lessons to prepare kids for the assignment didn't land. But, it's possible that some of the information soaked in. Focus on that. Focus on the wins. The losses are important too because there needs to be remediation. But, not everything was a loss, right?

Thinking back to those striving learners again (instead of clouding the paper with the wrong) shine light on what was done right. There may only be two or three things done right but hey, that's two or three things that a student learned. If you keep focusing on the gains, eventually you will find yourself surrounded by success instead of failure.

Forty-Four

WHAT YOU WEAR MATTERS

As unfortunate as this sounds, what you wear matters. Want to be treated as a boss? Dress like one. Want to be the cool, laid-back teacher? Dress like it. The kids notice. They see you, and your clothes are an extension of the human your kids try to figure out. Kids use clothes to express who they are, right? They assume it works the same for you. Even if it isn't accurate, they don't know it.

If you come into work looking like a hot mess, the students are going to assume that's how your classroom runs. And, doesn't it? If you come in a hot mess because your morning was hectic, doesn't that hectic morning usually bleed into your day because your lesson may not be as prepared as you would like or you're scrambling to make copies or your brain is preoccupied. If you look put together, the students will assume you actually *are* and class will run accordingly.

If you want to move up in your career, what you wear matters. Teachers have shown up to work in the *worst* outfits. Leggings, dirty sandals which had black toe imprints, sparkly club dresses that probably shouldn't have been worn even to nightclubs. Bad. Just bad. No matter how brilliant, talented, qualified a teacher might be for an administration position, it might not happen if your appearance isn't up to par. It might be harder to convince leadership to take you seriously when you wear a sequin club dress to school.

On Fridays, some teachers can wear jeans and a school T-shirt. If you struggle with classroom management, maybe don't partake in those first few weeks because the atmosphere in the class is more relaxed when you wear jeans. It could just be the Friday vibes, but maybe don't risk it at first. If you typically teach remedial students, you know it takes a few weeks for them to become familiar with the classroom expectations. Are you willing to jeopardize order for comfort? Not yet. Give it a few weeks.

However, comfort is incredibly important. You might not be your best self when you are self-conscious about an outfit or uncomfortable in the clothing you're wearing. If something is too tight and rolls up so you have to adjust it every two minutes, you're going to hate your day. Teachers do not have the time or brain power to be fidgeting with clothes. If your neckline dips too low for your comfort and you have to keep hiking it up, don't wear it. Be comfortable, but not in pajamas.

Invest in good professional clothing with maximum comfort even if they come from a resale shop. There are these work trousers for women that slip on like leggings. You would never know there is an elastic waist on these bad boys and the range of motion you will have in them make them feel like pajamas—but they aren't. You would never know. Find them and buy them in every color. They always fit, they always look nice and professional, and you will always be comfortable. There are ways to be comfortable and professional at the same time. Men, they have pants like this for you as well.

Teachers need to be able to bend down to help kids without worrying about a skirt that's too short or ripping the seam on a pair of too-tight pants (this has happened before). Teachers need to be able to lean over without worrying about an obscene amount of cleavage. You also might need to hide any stress sweat. The first few days or weeks can be sweaty times. The stress sweat might be a real problem for you like it is for so many other people. So, choose your shirts carefully. Wear ones that conceal. Loose sleeves or light colors with patterns usually work.

So, yes, comfort is important. But, shop strategically. You don't need to be in basketball shorts or leggings to be comfortable. And (this is a must), you have to wear a bra, ladies. Spend the money on a good one but you actually have to wear it. Or, at least wear shirts that conceal your bralessness effectively.

As unfortunate as it is, what you wear matters. Your clothes should be an extension of your personality, but should also be appropriate for the workplace.

Forty-Five

GOOD TEACHERS ARE ALWAYS STUDENTS

Something so wonderful about this career is the constant churning of new information in the brain. The educational climate is ever evolving. It is in the best interest of the teachers, and the students, for teachers to be willing to learn and change with that climate. Not adapting and evolving would be like wearing a fur coat from a northern state with snow down to Florida where the temperatures reach over 100 degrees. You will be uncomfortable, you could suffocate, and you will most definitely be cranky—with mostly everything.

Teachers need to be adaptable and that adaptability extends to their own personal growth and education. Not only do curriculums change, but state expectations change. Not only do these change, but kids change. You are not teaching the same kids who were being taught ten, fifteen, or twenty years ago. The climate is different and the teacher can either suffocate in the change of weather or they can change their clothes to be more comfortable . . . and pleasant.

Really, how many times can teachers teach the same, tired curriculum before they start to resent it? If teaching *Romeo and Juliet* one more time would be enough to induce a stroke, you probably need a change. Request to be moved to a different grade level.

With this shift, you will need to learn new texts. If making the jump from ninth grade to twelfth grade, not only do you need to learn the new curriculum and standards but you also need to learn different classroom management techniques. Those eighteen-year-olds are not the same as those thirteen-year-olds and should not be treated the same. They can vote, get tattoos, and work in bars. They are entirely different animals. Buy a book. Take some professional development courses. Adapt.

So, then what do teachers do when they need to teach material or skills they don't know? Each time you teach a new class, maybe tell the kids about it. Be honest that it's your first year and there's a learning curve that you need to conquer together.

Rarely will you be shunned by them for being new to the course. In fact, make them part of the learning process. Get them invested in this investigative process. Assign a project. Give each group of students a different sample essay and learn about the course expectations together.

It will be authentic, the students will see value in it, and it will save you a ton of time digging through twenty released student essays. Make them part of the learning process and model that learner-for-a-lifetime mentality.

It doesn't take additional degrees to learn and grow in your field. Oftentimes, your administration wants growth from you and will be willing to help. Find conferences to attend. It is doubtful you will be turned down when you ask to attend. You may need to fight a little for it, but do it. Fight. Convince them this is a learning opportunity that will benefit you and your students.

When you make a jump, like elementary to middle school, for example, see if there is a conference focusing on classroom engagement or any professional development that will help prepare you for that move. If the administration won't fund the conference, then your district might. There are funds for professional development, you just have to find them.

Even if you teach the same class every year for over a decade, switch it up and continue your own education. Find a conference or some professional development that incorporates art into the classroom, so instead of the typical project you might assign, you make it art based.

Learning new classroom strategies, curriculum, and projects is refreshing. Even though you might have new kids every year and *they* may not have done that research project, you have. A thousand times. Why not switch it up and see what new and exciting ideas or activities are out there? Teach a new novel, find a new podcast.

A free and highly recommended way to add fresh, new ideas and projects is to join a social media platform with teachers who teach similar classes. Become a member of about five different teacher groups and you will be surprised with the constant, new, and innovative ideas you might find.

How can teachers instill a love of learning into their students if they don't share that same passion? Change doesn't have to be scary. Change can be more of a metamorphosis, if you let it.

Forty-Six
DON'T LET THE DATA SCARE YOU

Whether you are a new teacher or a veteran teacher, student testing data can be confusing and sometimes a bit intimidating, but it doesn't need to be. Student data can come from various sources, but here are some of the most common data sources (table 46.1).

Table 46.1

Data Source	Information Type	Frequency
State Assessments or End of Course Exams	Summative Assessments (They test the sum of what a student learned in a year.)	Usually once per year per subject
Progress Monitoring	Formative Assessments (These are usually not taken for a grade, but rather are used to inform your instruction moving forward. They are based on what standards students are expected to have mastered by the end of the year.)	Three or four times a year and this is usually set by your school district or state
Unit Tests, Exit Tickets, Section Tests, etc.	Standards-Based Assessments (These assessments are usually graded and are based on standards being taught in the classroom. These are usually teacher-driven.)	Weekly (section tests), biweekly (unit tests), or sometimes daily (exit tickets)

Each of these data sources provide a glimpse into a student's academic progress at any given moment, and looking at all three types of data at once can provide a more complete picture of a student's academic growth over time. If any of these three data sources are missing, then there are going to be holes in the data you are using to inform your instruction. Yes, this data should be informing your instruction.

If a specific standard is being assessed on the state exam at the end of the year, say long-division, then you are going to want to assess how the student is doing with long-division throughout the year as you teach, reteach, and expand upon it. These mini-assessments and tests are going to be your standards-based assessments. If a student isn't grasping the concept in these assessments, then you know to keep working on this skill with this student.

Data might seem scary, but many Learning Management Systems or textbook publisher platforms have their own data points that can be quickly navigated. Most of the data is color coded in a way that is user-friendly: green=good scores, red=scores that need improvement. Many teachers find the information these programs offer incredibly helpful as they build their lesson plans and work to increase student achievement. To do this, they need a clear map of what skills students need. This map is usually found in the course standards and in the test item specifications for your state exam.

Once these two pieces are put into place, teachers work backward to determine just how a student learns these skills: what smaller skills need to be built and layered to scaffold this skill for students? Many students will need various exposures to skills and strategies in order to master them and obtain long-term retention, and the data is there to show you whether your teaching is having an effect.

Not only should the data let teachers know if their methods are working, but they should also let students know if they are learning. Students should be familiar with their own educational data.

It shouldn't be placed on a wall with race cars or sunflowers growing (because seriously, who wants to be the last race car or the shortest sunflower?) but a private, student-created bar graph can provide students with a snapshot of their own learning and growth. Break out the colored pencils and rulers—the more you have students chart their own successes and strivings, the more ownership they take on their learning, and the more invested they become. If your progress monitoring system doesn't show kids their data, that might be a great conversation to have with your students.

Analyzing data might seem scary, but it doesn't need to be. Ask a teacher near your room for help. Ask your administrator. Ask your data technician at your school, or even in your district. People will help, and the more frequently you look at the data, the less intimidating it becomes. Every student deserves the chance to learn and grow in their classrooms so it only makes sense to use data to make the most out of every available instructional minute.

Forty-Seven

POLISH YOUR DRAGON SCALES

Teachers need to have a balance between being sensitive sages and fierce warriors. They need to have empathy for their kids, people around the world, and fellow teachers. However, if they are too sensitive, this career will eat them alive.

This career leaves you vulnerable. Vulnerable to criticism from people all around you. The students have opinions about your ability to teach. Administrators literally evaluate your ability to teach. And even people in the community have a lot of opinions about what you should and should not teach.

As years of criticism come crashing down, teachers need ways to filter and evaluate. Some teachers give their students teacher evaluations each year, and, at first, for new teachers, their egos or self-esteem might not be able to handle it. If you fall into that category, then don't do it. Do not feel the need to ask your kids to evaluate your classes if you know you are going to take the criticism too personally. There's nothing wrong with avoiding these feelings for a while.

Now, some teachers love these evaluations and read them at the beginning of each school year. They have the ability to set aside their hurt feelings in order to do better. Neither teacher is the better teacher, it's all about your dragon scales, and they take time to grow.

Student evaluations can be powerful, but also incredibly hurtful. The trick is to ask questions carefully. Make sure they have to explain any issues they have.

Some questions you can ask:

1. "Which assignment or project did you enjoy the most? Be sure to explain why and whether or not you think next year's students would benefit from completing this assignment?" This type of question prompts them to immediately focus on the positive that happened in class. If several students picked the same project, that's a win. If they all left out that huge research project, maybe revisit it and revise it for next year.
2. "Do you think my grading policy was fair and equitable? Be sure to explain your answer and support it with specific examples." This gives students room to vent

their frustrations but does not offer room to specifically target you as a person. This is not your personality or necessarily your teaching style. Grading policies can easily be changed without hurt feelings.
3. "Do you think our texts were diverse enough? Explain. If not, which representation do you feel is missing?" This one is important. Teachers want their kids to feel included, represented, seen, heard. And, this is still about content and not teaching abilities. Hurt feelings can be avoided here.
4. "What is one thing you learned from this year that you think will be valuable in your future? Explain." Again, this is focusing on the positive. Take the popular answers and count that assignment as a win. If no one picked the unit on X, Y, and Z, maybe revisit it to make it more meaningful.
5. "What is one thing you would change about this class? Explain. Explain thoroughly. Don't just deliberately hurt my feelings." This one can get personal. This one can be eliminated. But, it does offer teachers the opportunities to make some changes for the better. See the chapter about fresh starts for more on this.

Getting these kinds of evaluations throughout the year might be helpful, too. Don't wait until the end of the year to find out students think sidewalk chalk (to be discussed in another chapter) is lame and not useful. After you try something new or are unsure about a certain assignment, survey the kids. This can be anonymous. You can draw a spectrum on your board and at one end, write "hated everything about it and saw no value" and on the other end write "I loved it and I think we should do it again because I learned so much." Then give them magnets when they walk in and ask them to place their magnet appropriately on the board based on their feelings.

Students can see what each other thinks, but you won't know who thinks what. Which, as teachers know, students are way more honest when their names aren't attached.

The point is that this feedback is valuable. Maybe you need to make the objective more clear? Maybe you need to choose a different culminating activity? Either way, take the feedback and evaluate how useful it is. Use your dragon scales as armor, but remember that dragons have soft underbellies that need protecting.

Section 9

INCREASING STUDENT ENGAGEMENT AND LEARNING

Forty-Eight
BACK TO THE BASICS

When the bucket and scissors and markers come out, students cheer. They. Cheer. Both six-year-old students and sixteen-year-old students ranging from remedial courses to college level get excited when the markers enter the agenda for the day. Even the students with ankle bracelets on because they're on house arrest get excited when they know the class is about to head back to the basics.

In an age with so much digital access, kids can forget what it was like to cut, color, and paste—especially the older ones. That tactile, hands cutting paper and gluing down pictures from a magazine, is not the same as copying and pasting a picture into a Google Doc. It's just not.

Kids like to cut, color, paste, design, create. That creative process can be a massive outlet for many of your kids. Even the kids who act too cool to care about sidewalk chalk get down on the concrete and draw a map of China's most lucrative trading routes. Let them make a mess. Let them talk to their friends while they cut, paste, and sort countries based on natural resources. Sure, you could give them a chapter to read, show them a map, give them a list, to show them natural resources but it doesn't have the same retention power as actually cutting and pasting and sorting.

Activate as many parts in the brain as you can. That's when kids are engaged and those are the assignments they remember.

When working on rhetoric basics: ethos, pathos, logos, a go-to assignment is cutting up magazine advertisements. Students have twenty minutes to find a set amount of advertisements that utilize all three appeals. Then, they choose a colorful sharpie (which is actually a fun process for them) and they annotate the advertisement identifying and explaining the appeals being used. Then, they evaluate the effectiveness. Even the striving students thrive.

This is an excellent scaffolding tool because they don't realize this is the first step to analyzing written arguments and they're just so engrossed in cutting, sorting, gluing, and annotating they don't realize actual learning is happening.

They giggle with their friends while doing this. They find advertisements for alcohol or tampons and they giggle and joke about how they are going to pull the

Absolut Vodka advertisement because it has all three appeals. Ha-ha. Well, actually, joke's on them because they just analyzed an extra advertisement. Ha-ha.

Sometimes, instead of taking traditional notes, pull out markers and have them sketchnote. Instead of words, have them illustrate the information. There are tons of online videos about how to do this. Show them a three-minute how-to video and let them try it. Triggering that part of the brain, especially if they don't typically draw or color when working on math or science, for example, excites them. Their excitement might be covered by groans of pretend protest, but those kids complaining are the first to pick out their favorite-colored markers.

School doesn't have to be so serious all the time. Even in classes where students are earning college credit, there is nothing wrong with coloring. They love it. Instead of writing an essay on the effects of deforestation in Africa, they could illustrate their essay. Or, instead of writing about bills becoming laws, they could sketchnote that process. The opportunities to create are endless.

Why can't they draw their notes on a history lecture instead of typical columned notes? Why can't they illustrate a word math problem in order to dissect it into its separate parts before trying to solve it? Or, turn the process of solving the problem into a comic strip? Of course, they can. And, the results might surprise you. Have them turn the lecture into a comic strip inserting their personal take on the information. These are actually hilarious.

The argument isn't to fully ditch computers and technology. In this digital age, the students need those technology skills and practice. And, the computers can also be engaging. However, not all students optimize their learning on computers and not all students learn better on paper. So, classrooms need to strike a balance to meet the needs of all kids. Because, regardless if they are sixth graders or twelfth, they are still kids. And, even if you prefer the computers, that doesn't mean the kids do.

Forty-Nine

GET 'EM MOVIN'

"If anyone draws a penis, we are coming back inside and writing five essays!"

This, unfortunately, might need to be your last instruction before you brave the scary world outside your classroom. Teachers don't usually travel farther outside their classrooms with their students once those students get into middle or high school. They certainly don't usually travel farther than the hallway because leaving the safety of their classrooms might make them feel vulnerable—more importantly, it leaves the students feeling exhilarated.

Students love to get out of the classrooms. It can be frightening, especially for new teachers, to venture out into the halls with twenty-five to thirty students because the teacher is clearly outnumbered. And, yes, it could go poorly.

But, it could also be great.

Give it a try. Give your students a chance.

There are a couple activities you can bring out into the hallway. To the displeasure of your custodial staff, you could use the windows as work space. If you have an indoor campus, you might have a set of windows somewhere in the school where students can work. Take your best whiteboard markers—the bright colorful ones that you might usually reserve for yourself, and let the students pick their color. You would be surprised how competitive students get over nice markers.

Put the students into teams, but be sure to assign their teams yourself whenever you leave the classroom because they can't be completely trusted; the students have their limits. The freedom of leaving the classroom coupled with their friends is really just asking for some kids to disappear or inappropriate things to be drawn on one of the windows or, one time, the floor (which did not erase as nicely as the markers on the windows). But anyway, yes, assign teams. Make those teams three people per window but really it depends on where you are in the school, how big the windows are, how many kids can fit in the space, etc. It just depends.

Once the teams are made, there are various activities you can do. Students can either plan for essays, answer questions, annotate something (poems, artwork, advertisements), work on math problems, plan out experiments, etc. The activities are endless. You can have them rotate windows every five minutes like stations. Once the work is finished, take a picture with your phone to grade the work and have the students erase the windows.

It doesn't really matter what you have them doing as long as they are moving. Hang up large pieces of paper throughout a hallway and have them do a silent discussion, but spread the papers out so they have to walk a bit to get to them (while still being supervised). Use large index cards and write questions on them that they need to answer and tape them up on the walls.

Make them move. Do anything. These kids sit for more hours a day than most people spend sleeping. It's crazy. Students get excited to leave the room for something new. Invest in a class set of clipboards. Have students trade their phones for a clipboard. This is key because the phones can stay locked in the classroom and they won't have them with them.

Always provide a hefty warning to your students before you try this for the first time. Warn them that if anyone (even one single person) embarrasses you or irreparably annoys you then you won't ever do this again and the entire class can spend eternity in those tiny desks. They usually don't want to screw up and usually keep each other in line.

Maybe don't attempt this in the early stages of school. You must assert your unquestionable dominance as alpha before you let the herd run free. They need a healthy fear of knowing that if they challenge the alpha they will lose and be ostracized from the remaining herd.

Teachers need to remember that the students are still kids and they like to get up and move around. Switch up the ways you practice with skills in your class. If something can be done in the hallway with a clipboard, go for it.

Fifty
SHOW STUDENTS THE WORK MEANS SOMETHING

Students are rather adept at identifying "busy work," and they don't appreciate it. If students are going to complete an assignment, it should build toward an end goal they recognize and perceive as important. Students and teachers alike should clearly understand the end goals and recognize the steps needed to achieve them. This is where an in-depth understanding of state standards and test item specifications can really help teachers, and students, to recognize the value in their work.

One way to make this connection clear for your students is to post daily objectives on the board in language students will understand. Don't write a standard number on the board—these don't mean anything to anyone. Even writing out the language of the standard isn't entirely clear for students because state standards are not always written with student consumers in mind. Turning the language of the standard into a SWBAT (Student Will Be Able To) statement is far easier for students to understand.

Using a grade nine/ten standard from the Common Core for ELA, multiple steps are required in order for students to be able to master this standard. Examine the difference in table 50.1.

Table 50.1

Common Core Standard: Taken from www.corestandards.org	CCSS.ELA-LITERACY.RL.9-10.3 Analyze how complex characters (e.g., those with multiple or conflicting motivations) develop over the course of a text, interact with other characters, and advance the plot or develop the theme.
SWBAT Statements:	• Students will be able to identify characters with conflicting motivations (complex characters). • Students will be able to analyze how complex characters change over the course of a story. • Students will be able to analyze how complex characters interact with other characters. • Students will be able to analyze how complex characters move the story forward. • Students will be able to determine the theme of a story. • Students will be able to analyze how complex characters develop the theme of the story.

Clearly, students will not be able to complete the tasks required for this standard in one class setting. Students might need multiple days or even weeks of working with just this one standard in order to be able to demonstrate mastery. There are six SWBAT statements in just this one standard. If students aren't told why they are learning how to determine if a character is complex, if they never see the language of the standard and the expectation or understand why it is relevant to them, then they might not have much buy-in to the process, and may miss out on all of the learning after the initial step.

Writing the SWBAT statement on the board is one way to get students to understand why the work matters, but there are other ways to get students to buy in as well.

1. Allow students to examine the test item specifications: there is no reason to hide public-knowledge information from your students. If questions on the state or national exam are weighted certain ways, explain the weighting system to kids. Give them a peek behind the curtain, let them know WHY they need to pay more attention to the questions weighted more heavily than others.
2. Attach SWBAT statements within the directions of assignments—give students goals for every task. There is no room for busy work if standards-based objectives are connected to every task.
3. Get students to buy into the test. Whether you are teaching third graders to read for the main idea or teaching high school students the complexity of physics, there are exams students need to take to prove proficiency, and students need to feel those tests hold value and merit, otherwise, none of the goals and objectives matter. Whether you agree with the test or not, whether you think the test is an accurate measure of a student's academic ability or not, you must sell the assessment to your students. They are going to follow your lead.

We need students to see the value in the work they complete. Elementary school students need to know it is preparing them for middle school. Middle school students need to see that the work is preparing them for high school. And high school students need to see that work will prepare them for their near-adult future. We need to make learning relevant for them. Without showing students the work matters, there isn't much incentive for them to complete it.

Fifty-One
MAKE IT YOURSELF

That whole mentality of *not reinventing the wheel* isn't necessarily true. Of course, people reinvented the wheel. Think about how many different versions of wheels there are. Each serves a different purpose, a different population. Think of tires. Some are best for snow, sand, mud, etc. Your lessons are the same. Not all wheels work for your climate. There's a reason you may not find the exact project you want for a unit you're working on in class. Because it doesn't exist. But, it should.

Trying to confidently teach someone else's brain power is actually problematic for a lot of teachers. It gives them horrible imposter syndrome. Teachers are way more passionate about their own projects than someone else's. This isn't intending to discredit all the amazing resources out there made by teachers, some of those will be exactly what you want, but a lesson is more meaningful when it comes from you. When it comes from your own brain and serves your very specific purpose.

If you don't have a specific vision and you just need an assignment to get the job done, then those premade lessons online will do the trick. But, if there is something specifically magical you are trying to do with your kids, take the time to make the project you envision. You might find something similar online, sure, but it isn't quite what you were hoping for. Take the time to create it. You will have more stake in the results, you will be more excited when you present it to your kids, and you will be able to use it for years.

When you create these handouts, projects, reference sheets, etc., make sure you design them for longevity and adaptability:

- Keep the information a little vague so it can be applied across units—but not too vague that the kids don't know what to do. For example, let's say you want them to explore the characterization in *Life of Pi*. Instead of specifically asking how the sinking of the ship affects his religion, you might ask how a major tragedy affects the character's beliefs. Or, how has the character's main conflict changed how he views the world.

Or, if wrapping up a unit in your textbook, instead of asking content-specific questions, make them broader. Ask about the biggest take-aways, most significant information or ideas, or map the overall cause and effect or problem and solution. This way, you can reuse this assignment for any unit you might teach in the future.
- Keep it in a document that can be easily edited and modified. If you only save the PDF version, you will have to recreate it if you want to reuse it for something else.

There is a huge teaching community who offers tons of great material. Teachers are typically huge proponents of the mentality that it takes a village, however, as known from experience, there is more passion over the content, project, assignments, or assessments, if they are designed by the teacher teaching them. These resources can be beneficial and can save you a ton of time. However, taking the time to make the perfect test or project will be time well spent. Brainstorming the project with your kids might help cut down on some of the prep. Have them help you create the criteria, expectations, rubric, and product.

Having kids help will increase their buy-in as well as yours.

Yes, it's time-consuming and teachers are all busy—very busy. But, remember that the snow tires a teacher uses in a northern state will not work on the roads in Florida. The wheel had to be reinvented (or differentiated) in order to meet the needs of a different climate. Teacher's classes are temperamental, and you might need your own wheel to make it through your specific terrain successfully.

Fifty-Two

STUDENT CHOICE

Remember those classes in school (and this doesn't include college classes) where the teacher would stand in front of the room and impart their wisdom upon you for the entire class period? No? That sounds about right. That's probably because kids have attention spanning about three minutes. They are not paying attention to you talking *at* them for forty-five minutes. Teachers are lucky if they can hold their students' for the five minutes it takes to explain an assignment. And, even then, you better have it written down somewhere where they can reference those directions fifteen minutes after you deliver them.

It can be frustrating to have to cater to this new generation. Once upon a time, students had a higher attention span. But, with the overloading of stimulus within the world today, this just isn't the case anymore. Teachers have to compete with so many other entertainment avenues to hold the attention of their students. It's hard to compete with an infinite amount of sixty-second videos students binge watch. Teachers can either fight against that—and lose. Or, they can adapt, change, and grow.

If students are not interested, assignments won't get done. Or at least they won't be done with quality. It's that simple. Many students would rather fail the assignment than do something they really don't want to do. This isn't good job training. Teachers know it isn't. However, won't they get choices in the real world? Don't want to do your own taxes? Fine. Hire someone. Don't want to grocery shop? OK. There's a way around it too. Your students live in a world of convenience and if an assignment is inconvenient for them, well, it might not get done.

The problem is, teachers are still held accountable for student learning. So, they need to combat this apathy and make them invested in what they're doing. One way to increase this buy-in from the students is to give them choices.

If you can evaluate the effectiveness of a lesson in different ways, then why not allow students to show their understanding in one of those different ways? Can they write an essay, complete a one pager, or make a video, and regardless of which route they choose, they can show you they learned what they needed to learn? Sure, so why not give them the choice?

Giving these options isn't as difficult as it sounds. You wouldn't have to make four different rubrics if you offer four different types of projects. If the rubric is content and standards focused, one rubric can apply to all projects. Now, directions might need to be differentiated, but, make those directions once so you can use them for years (see the chapter about making it yourself).

Here are some ideas for choice projects:

- Essays
- One pagers
- Sketchnotes
- Videos
- Slideshows
- Poster Boards (digital or paper)
- Websites
- Also, you can open it up to students to make a proposal. Hear them out, make them defend their choice, and approve or deny accordingly.

By having students choose, they take ownership over the project. When students hit a figurative wall in a traditional assignment, they quit. However, with the ability to switch mediums, more students switch project types than quit it entirely.

One major challenge to this ability to choose is the timing. An essay might not take as long to complete as a video. It is recommended that you choose three options for the kids. When choosing those options, make sure the timeline will be similar for all three. Also, you can provide your students with a blank calendar. If they have five class periods, as an example, to complete this project, then have them map out the steps they need to take on those five days. They can show you what they plan to accomplish on each day in order to meet the deadline. If you have time, grade each step as it's completed to cut down on grading time. There's a chapter about this as well.

Student choice empowers students to demonstrate their learning in a way that is meaningful to them. You are battling attention spans whittled down by quickly consumed social media, you want your students battling with you, not against you.

Fifty-Three
LET YOUR KIDS STRUGGLE

Teaching can feel a bit like being a lighthouse. Master teachers shine through the darkness, illuminating the path so students can traverse forward with the knowledge they need to make safe and smart decisions. Quite often at the start of the year you will need to be a lighthouse in your room. But even beyond the start of the year, your lighthouse light needs to shine brightly each time a new skill or concept is introduced. You need to light the path, offer the knowledge, warn against potential problems so little learners don't crash their academic boats against the rocky shore.

But, there are times, many times in fact, you will need to dim your lights. You will need to transition from being a lighthouse to being a fire tower. As a fire tower, you allow students to work on their own. You allow them to struggle a bit, to play around with problems, to make missteps, secure new paths, and forge a new trail. You don't need to interfere.

Teachers need to let kids struggle. This is where the learning happens. This is where kids realize they have made mistakes and where they learn to fix them.

Teachers are there to watch for the fires. Teachers need to see the smoke, calculate if it is a small, controlled burn, or a gigantic raging fire. Students are going to have small metaphorical fires as they work, these mark the trail of their learning. But the big fires, the ones seen from the fire tower, need intervention. Those need to be put out.

Kids shouldn't get frustrated to the point of quitting while you let them struggle. It is a delicate balance, different with each student and with each new skill. It takes knowing your kids to know when to step in, when to ask if the student would like some feedback, when to show a few more samples if there are more than three or four fires threatening the forest of the classroom.

Teachers need to know what signals to look for so they can tell when the fire is burning out of control and students are giving up the fight. Teachers need to know when to intervene. This can look different depending on the age of the student you teach, but here are some signals students give when they are about to go up in flames:

- Putting a head down
- Pulling out a cell phone
- Disrupting a neighbor
- Taking an exceptionally long bathroom break
- Sighing or making frustrated noises
- Head in hands
- Staring out the window
- Trying to copy from a classmate

Allowing students the opportunity to struggle can help make them more resilient and competent learners, but letting them transition from struggle into heavy frustration can have the opposite effect, making them resistant to trying in the future. You might need to switch from being a fire tower to lighthouse and back many times in a week or even a class period depending on the ability level of your learners and the skills you are teaching, and it takes time to learn when to transition back and forth, but knowing the transition needs to happen is a crucial step. You could consider smaller-scale interventions like:

- Scaffold instruction right from the start using the I do, we do, you do method of gradual release where you model an activity, then have students work either with you or with a group to complete a similar activity, and then students try it out independently.
- Model one of the questions from the assignment on the board for the class.
- Ask a student volunteer to come up to the board to demonstrate one question.
- Circulate the room and independently work with students as you see them struggle.
- Partner students up for a two-minute debrief on the assignment where they share their work and learn from one another before continuing their independent work. (These can be unplanned and implemented as needed.)

Teachers can't spend too much time in either phase, but it takes time and relationship building to become a lighthouse keeper, fire spotter, and master educator. Don't panic if you get the balance wrong at the start. Just keep spotting those fires and leading those boats to shore.

Fifty-Four
HOLY SH*% CLASS ENDED EARLY, NOW WHAT?

Sometimes, regardless of the lessons you plan and the extension activities you have in place, class just ends early. It happens. Even on these days, keep those kids busy and learning. Use the time left at the end of the period for academic purposes. Working bell to bell shows students you value their time and you value their learning. Do *not* let them line up at the door early. Ever. When they line up at the door early, the message is that your class time doesn't matter, and that is never the message kids should get about class time.

Anticipating students might end up with extra time at the end of lessons, it is helpful to have some exercises and tools ready to go for such an instance. Below are a few useful tools for when there is spare time at the end of the period:

- *Beach ball review:* If you have a beach ball blown up under your desk, this can be pulled out whenever there are spare minutes at the end of a period and you can use it as a review activity. Regardless of what you are studying, whether it be the play *Hamlet* or the properties of thermodynamics, you can toss the ball into the class and the first person to catch it has to give a fact about what you are learning. Then they pop the ball into the air and the next person to remain seated but catch it has to say another fact, and so on and so on. It is a fun way to end a class, and it keeps the kids in their seats and learning.
- *Exit tickets:* Exit tickets are quick check-ins related to content providing a non-intimidating way for students to show what they know. These are usually one or two questions long and can be multiple-choice or open-ended. They can be related to a skill you are currently teaching or a previously taught skill. If you have these prepared on a slideshow or index cards ready to put under a projector, you won't have to think of them on the spot, you can have them ready to project at a moment's notice.
- *Quick Content Summaries:* Asking students to summarize a concept in ten words or less (summarize on a dime), is another way to enhance learning at the end of a lesson. It helps if students write their summary on a sticky note because then, on

their way out of the classroom, they can stick their response to the classroom door or window or back wall. It doesn't need to be formally turned in as an assignment unless you want it to be.
- *Vocabulary review:* Reviewing vocabulary can help students master big concepts they need to know in order to move forward in the curriculum. These could be more generic academic words such as *analyze* or *contrast* or they could be content-specific words such as *theme* or *climate*.
- *Background work:* If students always have a project running in the background of your classwork, they can always fall back on this work when there is time at the end of class. For example, if you have students researching a famous mathematician in preparation for a presentation at the end of the quarter, they could spend time researching if the lesson finishes early. Students could write in a journal or read a book on the topic you are studying or even go back and revise work they have already completed (like essays). Whatever the kids are working toward as a larger goal can fit into this space.
- *Objectives check in:* Consider using this extra time to check in with students on how they feel they are progressing toward the unit or lesson objectives. Have them write a reflection on which skills they feel confident about, which might need more work, and ask them to cite specific evidence to back up their assessments of their progress.

None of these closing activities need to be taken for a grade. You don't need to put more work on yourself to enter assignments in the gradebook. They are for you to get a pulse on your kids, see where they are landing, see where they might need additional support, and keep them learning. Allowing them to play on their phones or line up at the door at the end of a lesson does none of this. Using those few minutes wisely sets the stage for learning and keeps the stage set all year long.

Section 10

INCORPORATING READING AND WRITING

Fifty-Five
READING ISN'T JUST FOR ENGLISH CLASS

This chapter is going to make someone mad. Get ready. States and education gurus seem to switch positions every few years on these two statements: sometimes "every teacher is a reading teacher" and sometimes "not every teacher is a reading teacher."

Even if a secondary content-area teacher isn't teaching phonics to their students, even if a biology teacher isn't teaching the main idea or theme, every teacher is a reading teacher. The content in every subject area needs to be read with a specific set of skills.

Reading like a mathematician is different from reading like a historian. Students need to be taught how to read in each respective discipline by masters in those fields. An English teacher may not know how to best read as a scientist, but the science teacher will. There are specific strategies to use when reading a lab report just as there are specific strategies to use when reading a poem, just as there are specific strategies for reading a word problem.

Each discipline has its own reading rules. Students won't be able to read their textbooks or pass their state exams without knowing how best to read the content. For example, reading the content of a science textbook varies drastically from reading in a math textbook, which varies drastically from reading in an English textbook.

There are some discipline-agnostic strategies students can employ to help them read actively and think critically about what they read as they read it. The strategies below are only a few of literally *hundreds* of strategies you can use to engage students in active reading regardless of discipline or course.

Pre-Reading: Setting the Stage for Critical Thought:

- *Beach Ball Discussions:* Prepare a current, topic-relevant, and open-ended discussion question(s) display on the board. Students then stand in a circle (move those desks out of the way) and allow the students to toss the ball to one another, responding to the discussion questions as they catch the ball.

- ○ For example, before beginning a unit on the causes of global warming, you could post the following questions to the class:
  1. What kinds of pollution do you think cause the most damage and why?
  2. Why do you think scientists worry about the environment?
  3. Why do you think the state thinks it is important for us to learn about climate change in this class?
- *Anticipation Chart:* In an anticipation chart, students are provided a list of statements, some true, some false, some personal, and students have to write in a chart whether they agree or disagree with the statement. Then, at the end of the lesson or unit, they go back to the chart and see if their thoughts have changed.

DURING READING: READ ACTIVELY AND THINK CRITICALLY

- Students should highlight main claims and supporting evidence as they read. Then, they should write questions in the margins. A question that can really get students thinking uses the stem, "Would _____ agree?". Students insert a noun into the blank—either the name of a group, organization, or specific person. By questioning claims and evidence from this outsider perspective and anticipating arguments, students are thinking critically about the concept being explored in the reading and they are also actively engaged in the reading itself.

POST-READING: APPLYING CRITICAL THINKING

- *Class Discussions:* Using those same questions from the beach ball activity or the statements from the anticipation guide as starting points, have students engage in small group discussions. Keep the discussions short and targeted so students don't stray from the topic at hand, but you can also ask them to address what from the reading they found most shocking, what they found to be most controversial, and ask them to discuss which nouns they put in their active reading questions. Oftentimes those questions from the margins of the reading can be enough to spark a weighty discussion among students.

Regardless of how many pre, during, and post reading activities you have planned for your kids, know they will be most actively engaged when the topic they are reading about connects to the immediate world around them—their community, their family, their school. Reading and writing should be taught cross-discipline so students can think critically about the world around them when teachers aren't there to guide them.

Fifty-Six
GET THEM WRITING

Writing does not have to solely live in the English class. In fact, it shouldn't.

Students need as much practice communicating their thoughts as possible. Remember when you used to pass paper notes to your friends in class? Those days are long gone and now student communication to their friends consists of poop emojis and memes.

All teachers need to work together to bridge this communication gap. If students only practice writing in their English class then they only associate communication with English class and that's problematic. Teachers try to convince them they need to practice communicating effectively because eventually they will be tiny adults, then real adults, and teachers need to make sure their students will not only survive the working world, but thrive within it. Students don't always believe good communication skills and their future endeavors connect. It's mind blowing.

Every class offers complex topics that invite great opportunities for students to write. When understanding a complex math problem, why not have the students write out the process to solve it? By breaking it down and being able to effectively communicate the process, they will increase their own understanding as well. And, you don't need to be an English teacher to be able to grade this. Have them swap their writing and copy the instructions verbatim to see if the process is correct.

When teaching public speaking, give students a picture and a partner. One partner has a marker and a dry-erase board the other has the picture. They sit back to back. The partner with the picture has to describe the picture without saying what it is. The partner with the marker has to draw it, exactly as it is described. This is hilarious and perfect for practicing descriptive communication and would be a great way to introduce writing into classes with processes.

There is also a lot of power in creative writing. In English courses, having students write a journal entry from the perspective of someone in one of their novels can be great for evaluating their understanding of characterization. Teachers don't need to give them a 100-question multiple-choice test to make sure they understand the complexity of the characters. They also don't need to give them a formal essay. How boring.

Other ways writing can be incorporated into curriculum:

- *Journaling:* Students can write a journal entry from the point of view of a character in a novel, play, short story, etc. Or, for history class, they can write a journal entry for someone famous they're learning about. Or, the journals can be reflective. At the end of each unit or lesson, say for a math class, students can reflect on what they learned, understand, and need more help with. They can simply free-write for three minutes wrapping their heads around the concepts just taught. This could apply to any class.
- *Genre Switching:* Have them re-create something using a different genre—have them turn a famous painting into a poem or short story. Or, have them turn a short story into song lyrics or a pitch for a potential movie. Or, they can turn a significant moment in history into a short story or a movie pitch.
- *Pen Pals:* Students can write letters to students in a different class period or who have a different math, English, art, or history teacher and write about the concepts being taught, their understanding of it, and their likes and dislikes. Then, swap letters and respond!
- *Writing Contests:* Students love these. Find free writing contests relative to what you are learning and have them enter. There are hundreds of free writing contests out there relative to all subject matters. Oftentimes, there are cash prizes for these free contests. And, it could give them something to discuss in their college admittance essays.

Get them to write more. Teachers can evaluate student understanding of the content being taught in more ways than a multiple-choice test. Even if the writing is purely reflective, this will benefit the students and increase their learning. It's worth the time taken from class to have them work on this reflective and communicative process. The grading doesn't have to be wild. Have them meet a word count. Did they write 100 words? Are they on task? Cool, "A"s for everybody.

Section 11

CROSSING THE DIGITAL DIVIDE

Fifty-Seven

INCORPORATING TECHNOLOGY

Aside from the standard Learning Management Systems such as Canvas, Schoology, or Google Classroom, there are other types of technology designed to enhance the learning experience and create engaging platforms for students to display their work, research, and communicate with one another. These platforms are meant to boost engagement in academic activities, but should be incorporated with intention and purpose.

As you create lessons and decide how to present material to your students as well as how you want students to demonstrate mastery of content, you may want to consider using the following technologies in your rooms to enhance the learning experience.

- *Interactive Discussion Platforms:* Online discussion platforms live within most Learning Management Systems, and they allow students to interact with their peers outside of the school day so they can share thoughts on what they are reading or studying. If students are in the same room with one another, a verbal discussion is best, but what if students are shy and refuse? They miss out on the learning opportunity that occurs within a classroom discussion. By hosting the discussion digitally, all students can participate equally.
- *Video Recording/Sharing:* Creating short, informal videos like those found on Flipgrid or inside Learning Management Systems allow students to respond to texts in authentic ways extended beyond writing. You will get to see a student's personality shine through more in a sixty-second video responding to an article on global warming than you will reading a short response they wrote. The content is the same. The learning is the same. The delivery is what changes.
- *Gamification:* Any time you are able to turn a review activity into a game, kids are more engaged. Whether they are six or sixteen, students enjoy competition. Gamified platforms for review such as Kahoot.com can target specific content and increase engagement. Plus, these are great for providing immediate feedback.

While knowing what tools to incorporate is helpful, it is also helpful to know when to incorporate new technology and how to stay in control of it.

- *Be certain to incorporate technology into your room slowly:* Allow students to learn, practice, and get comfortable with a platform or tool before you introduce them to another.
- *Match the right tool with the right outcome/expectation:* Don't expect dissertation quality work from a video. Match the tone to the product.
- *Don't expect the kids to just know the platform tools or the rules:* Be explicit. Teach these soft skills before you can teach or assess content through them.
- *Don't overuse it:* Unless you are teaching in a situation where full tech immersion is expected (like during a pandemic or in a tech-based school model) technology should enhance learning, should be an engagement tool—not the only tool.
- *Don't overdo it:* Try not to use fifteen different online platforms. Stick to five.

While technology can enhance the ways teachers communicate information with students and parents, it cannot replace the relationship that teachers foster with students. The field of education cannot allow the teacher, the expert in the room, to fade into the background of technology just for progress' sake. Relationships and academic engagement aren't dependent upon the employment of technology in classrooms, they are dependent upon teachers.

Fifty-Eight
LET YOUTUBE HELP

You do not need to know everything. You might feel pressured to know it all, but that is an *impossible* goal. Educators need to know their standards and their content, but once they stretch beyond this—when students start asking questions, when a text stretches outside your comfort zone, it is acceptable to answer a student's question with, "I'm not certain, let's find out." But then, you really have to follow through.

If you want to find out together, have the kids do a little research—four or five minutes is usually all it will take to answer the question, report out, and move on with the lesson (This is a great chance to talk to kids about reliable sources as well).

If you are researching a topic more complex than you are comfortable explaining, start with YouTube. Seriously. YouTube is full of mindless entertainment, but it is also full of incredible resources such as documentaries and lectures from other professionals who are teaching students from across the world. You can lean on experts. You can admit you don't have every answer to every question. You should strive to have many of the answers, but certainly not all of them.

YouTube videos can be engaging introductory tools as well. If you are teaching a unit about the Roaring Twenties, you might want to look up a video about the time period so students can have visuals for what they will be learning. By activating this background knowledge, you are building students a scaffold to help them as you move through the unit. This video can be delivered in class whole group or through your school's Learning Management System as homework, depending on the dedication and home situations of your students.

As helpful as YouTube can be as an educational tool, there are some potential concerns you need to consider before you show a video to your students.

1. *Ads:* If you have been bathing suit shopping online lately, or you have been researching mixed drinks to make for a summer barbeque, then your ads on YouTube might not be appropriate for students to see. YouTube tracks your internet browsing and tends to offer you advertisements leaning toward your interests. It is best to not use your work computer for any non-work-related internet browsing

so the ads showing up on your work-account YouTube will be generic and school-appropriate.
2. *Questionable Content:* You must *always* preview the entire video, even if you are only showing a snippet. This is because a student might be curious about the video and want to watch the rest later, or they might tell their parents they watched the video, and the parents don't know which part you showed. It is best to just ensure the entire video is school appropriate.
3. *Reliable Source:* Ensure that the channel/producers where you pull content from is a reputable and unbiased media source. Just as we want our students to check for reliable sources, we want to do so as well.

Incorporating YouTube into your lessons can be done quickly and easily and can genuinely increase engagement. Here are a few tips for when you might consider intentionally incorporating YouTube into your classes:

- *To introduce a skill:* If you are teaching students about volcanic eruptions, a compilation video of real eruptions from around the world would be an engaging way to get students invested in the unit.
- *To practice a skill:* If students are learning about identifying themes, before they dive into a short story or novel, have them practice by watching short, animated films on YouTube. There are many complex, animated, award-winning short films worthy of literary analysis (this is a natural scaffold for students before diving into literature).
- *To assess students:* If students are working on a project requiring a presentation, have them create their own YouTube video they could add to the YouTube universe (with parent permission, of course). Having students produce their own academic video gives them a genuine audience for their work and a sense of pride in what they accomplished.

If you want to enhance your incorporation of videos in the classroom, there are online platforms that allow teachers to embed questions into their videos (Edpuzzle.com is one of them), and adding questions to videos is an interactive and engaging way to use YouTube content to create independent work for your students.

Fifty-Nine
KEEP IT PG

As hard as you try, not every day will be an observation-worthy day. Some days, you will need to catch up on the grading. Some days, you aren't going to be feeling your tip-top best. Some days, the kids are over it. Some days, you will be over it. Movies were made for these days.

As long as you can connect the movie to your content, toss a few standards at it and make them stick, and it doesn't happen too often, you get a pass. You are a teacher, not a robot. Every day won't be perfect, and that is okay. Give yourself the grace to get beyond such an unrealistic expectation.

Knowing you might show a movie at some point, there *are* some ground rules.

1. Connect the movie to content. Discuss with your students why they are watching and what they should be hoping to gain.
2. Keep the film PG. Even if it is a documentary and it isn't rated, you will know if it crosses the PG line. Even if the child watching is seventeen, don't venture into PG-13 ratings.
3. Don't break copyright laws.
4. Ensure you don't offend anyone:
   - Violence—not just gore, but anything that might be hard to watch. Not just physical, but also verbal or societal.
   - Themes—make sure themes match your teaching philosophy. You don't necessarily want to promote vigilante justice. Or, be sure to offer a disclaimer.
   - Romance—not just sex scenes, but some heavy make-out scenes are just icky to watch in class.
   - Diversity. Watch out for older films and their treatment of culturally diverse peoples. Some older films handle diversity poorly. People are missing faces, or are horribly misrepresented, and it isn't even always race. Even if this isn't the point of the film, just an unfortunate symptom of the ignorance of the time period, this isn't a message you want to subliminally send your kids.

5. Preview the ENTIRE film first. Whether you are using YouTube, a DVD, or an old VHS tape, be certain you know what happens during every single moment of the film. In Zeffirelli's version of *Romeo and Juliet*, Juliet exposes her bare breasts to the screen and Romeo shows his bare bottom. If you aren't aware it is coming, this scene can cause a stir both with the students in the room and with the parents afterward.
6. NEVER leave a movie with a substitute. You should always have specific substitute plans prepared (it is just courteous) and students don't watch the film the way they would if you were in the room anyway. Substitutes are rare golden beings who need to be cherished and protected. Leave them good lessons. Save the movies for another time.

There are many ways to show a film, or portions of a film, and make it genuinely academic and engaging. Some strategies for this include:

- Incorporate snippets of film into your course to introduce content, YouTube works great for this. You can use these snippets to introduce concepts or to assess (see the chapter titled "Let YouTube Help" for more specifics).
- Watch a film or play adaptation after reading a novel allows students to note various changes from the original text to the adaptation, which allows students to engage in discussion, about why the director made some of the choices he or she did. Students have a chance to consider time frame, target audience, medium limitations, etc.
- Choose a film offering two opposing views on an issue and have students track claims and counterclaims to determine whose argument is strongest.
- Use documentaries to introduce historical or scientific topics to students before they read about them in their textbooks.
- Connect history and science to literature through documentaries in order to build background knowledge before reading, especially if what is being read is historical fiction.
- Choose films where a fictional president gives a speech. Have students re-watch the speech scene a few times and discuss what rhetorical strategies the screenwriters included that made the speech effective (or not). Fictional presidents give some pretty moving silver-screen speeches, and people rarely get political over a fictional president.

Not every film experience in your classroom needs to be considered an "off" day. Films can be incredibly educational and can be connected to almost any content area when approached thoughtfully, as long as you keep it PG.

Do you like your job? Good. Preview the material you show in class.

Section 12

CREATING AND MAINTAINING YOUR WORK–LIFE BALANCE

Sixty
KNOW YOUR LIMITS

One of the possible reasons the teaching industry loses so many first-year teachers is because new teachers take on too much, try to do too much, try to prove too much. Their passion for the profession can easily make their eyes bigger than their stomachs . . . or, in this case, their shoulders.

Teachers like to be involved in things that *matter* and make a difference. First year teachers might be the most eager because they are so excited to finally be in the classroom. However, it is quickly learned that we can't do *all* the things. Teachers literally can't do all the things.

The most important skill a teacher can learn, and the sooner they learn this the better, is the ability to say "no." When you know you have reached your limit, you have to be able to say no when someone else tries to lay something else on your shoulders.

Teachers are not martyrs. You don't have to be overworked and overburdened to be considered a good teacher. In fact, aren't many teachers lackluster teachers when they're overworked and overstressed? There's only so much responsibility a person can reasonably handle, and it is imperative you know your limits.

Here are some ways you can turn down additional responsibilities without sounding like you aren't a team player:

- "Hmm, that sounds interesting, and I appreciate you thinking of me, but I don't think I would be the right fit for that." They don't need to know your time is more valuable and that's why it wouldn't be a good fit.
- "I appreciate the offer but I think with X, Y, and Z on my plate I might not have the time that project deserves." This way you remind them you already have a thousand things you volunteered for so they don't think you're just avoiding extra work.
- If something genuinely does sound like something you want to do but you don't know if you can swing it yet, tell them: "That does sound like something I might be interested in, but I would need to look at the criteria (or expectations or description) before committing. Can I get back to you in a few days with an answer?" This

way, you buy yourself some time to really reflect on whether or not you want this additional task. Then, when you turn them down, if you turn them down, at least you thought it over and gave them that consideration. However, don't make them wait a few days if you know the answer is a hard no. That would be rude.

There's no shame in saying no. You just need to do it respectfully and professionally. And, if you are interested in taking on something extra, be sure to know where to seek help in those additional roles. Chances are, you have district curriculum specialists, academic coaches, family engagement coordinators, or other committees within your school system who might be willing to assist.

It is very important to point out that there are some things you cannot say no to. Those three suggestions will only work for additional roles and responsibilities.

What you can say no to:

- Sponsoring clubs
- Coaching sports
- Heading committees (although be careful saying no because they look for this when offering promotions)
- Participating in committees
- Teaching summer school
- Proctoring weekend ACT/SAT
- Anything else that extends beyond your contract hours

What you can't say no to:

- Proctoring school-based tests, like state assessments
- District initiatives that require trainings
- School initiatives, like door duties or hall monitoring
- IEP or 504 meetings
- Faculty or department meetings
- Data days

It is encouraged to get involved in the schools. That's what makes your school more of a community than a place to work. However, carrying giant boulders on your shoulders when everyone else is carrying normal-sized rocks could easily leave you feeling bitter and burned out.

Sixty-One
ALLOW YOURSELF TIME TO RECHARGE

You are not on call and you do not get paid to work at home. Let's hear that again. You do not get paid to work at home. This is not condemnation, more like an intervention. Tons of teachers bring work home. But, you should always remember that every time you bring schoolwork, anywhere *beyond* school, you are not getting paid. So make sure the sacrifice is worth it.

Is it worth it to you to be prepared for the upcoming week? If so, instead of scrambling around Monday morning trying to prepare for classes, you might prep Sunday night. Is that peaceful Monday morning worth it to you? If so, carry on. Yes, you will be working for free to be less stressed on Monday morning. That might be worth it to you. However, if spending your entire Saturday grading essays isn't worth it to you, then don't grade them. This is absolutely OK. The essays can wait.

You have to figure out what your time is worth. If grading 150 multiple-choice questions isn't worth sacrificing your Tuesday evening, then don't do it. No one will say you're a bad teacher because you don't stay up until 9 p.m. grading work. And, if they do, they clearly need to reassess their teaching philosophy. No one will ask you in an interview how many hours you spend outside your contract hours working. Never. There are no trophies for unpaid overtime.

Your time is precious. Your time is your own. You have to find that hard line where work is shut down. This is important for self care. This is important for your family.

This is easier said than done. Of course. Teachers always have a thousand things to do and are never caught up. However, deciding which tasks happen on your own time is imperative to a healthy work/life balance. Sometimes, working from home is just unavoidable. If that's the case, decide what is worth your time.

Here's some ways to help determine what comes home and what doesn't:

- If you need to plan a lesson, is the time you are taking from home worth the sacrifice? Will planning for free help alleviate some stress for you? Or, can you set aside some time where you are getting paid to make some lessons?

- Will grading those assignments bring you joy, making the time you are sacrificing worth it? If not, do not bring it home.
- Is it something you can spread out throughout the week? Meaning, can you set aside about ten minutes each morning or evening to get through a small stack of grading? Sacrificing a few minutes here and there doesn't seem as bad as sacrificing your entire Sunday. Grading a few assignments while your photocopies are going through, or while you wait for your coffee to brew is an easy way to slip in some multitasking.
- Can you grade that assignment by the pool or on the porch? That would make it less awful. There's nothing wrong with bringing work to a restaurant so you can enjoy a nice dinner while grading. Just don't go to a bar. That would be bad.
- For summer: Are you teaching something new? Do you need to become an expert in something new so that you don't feel like a bumbling idiot for the entire school year? That's fair. Bring that material home, if you must. Refer to the chapter about always being a student for more on this topic.

In an ideal world, work could be completely separated from home. But, that isn't always reality. When the two cannot be separated and your world will fall apart if you do not bring X, Y, and Z home, then fine, bring it home. But, make sure it is worth it.

Sixty-Two

KNOW YOUR CONTRACT

Teachers work hard. Really hard. Many teachers overload their hours—how else do lesson plans get written and emails sent and copies made and essays graded? When you are at school, the kids need you, but so many other tasks need to be accomplished in order to help the kids. Because this is the norm, many teachers are overextended, overplanned, and overstressed.

The first thing you should do when you are hired as a teacher is to learn your contract. Know when you are to report to school, what time you can leave, how often to update your gradebook, what the policies are for dealing with parents, all of it. Read it.

Then, when it comes to your contract hours, try to stick to them. Obviously, you won't always be able to do this. You might be tempted to see your student's basketball game because she invited you and you want to show support. You might be tempted to spend the extra twenty minutes after school working on the best lesson for the next day because you know your kids will love it. You might be tempted to grade the papers the night before grades are due. Just remember, all of this would happen outside of contract hours and you are not obligated to work outside your contract.

You are a human, not a robot. You have a life, you have interests beyond your classroom (and if you don't, you should work on developing some). You need to cook dinner and exercise and read for fun and binge watch shows for entirely too many hours and ride bikes and go for walks and enjoy sunsets—all the things that bring you joy that do NOT involve your classroom or your students. You need to shut it off and walk away, and do it as often as you can as close to your contract hours as you can.

Knowing your contract moves so far beyond just knowing your contractual work hours. Find your contract on your district's website (usually under the Human Resources page or tab) and as you read through it, reference the list below, answer the questions, and perhaps place the page number in your contract where these gems of information live.

CHAPTER SIXTY-TWO

- What is the time frame you have to respond to parent phone calls and emails?
  _____
  _____

- How is your evaluation calculated?
  _____
  _____

- What is in your code of ethics?
  _____
  _____

- What are your certification and recertification requirements?
  _____
  _____

- What are your professional development requirements?
  _____
  _____

- What is and is *not* public record in your email communications and other forms of communication?
  _____
  _____

- What information about students can you and can you not share, and with whom?
  _____
  _____

- What is the faculty dress code at your school site? Is it different on teacher work days than days with students?
  _____
  _____

- What is the protocol for applying for different positions within your district?

- What are the policies for assigning grades to students?

- What are the policies for updating grades in the gradebook?

- How does your district handle personal leave/sick days/maternity leave/family medical leave?

- What is your salary and pay schedule?

- What role does the union play in your contract?

- What are your benefits and retirement?

- What is the policy for handling money?

- What are your district's technology policies?

  _____

  _____

This chapter may take a bit of frontloading to fill in the questions, but once you have this completed, it will serve as an invaluable reference for you as you continue your teaching career. It is worth the time investment.

Sixty-Three

CENSOR YOUR SOCIAL MEDIA

Once you become a teacher, your bathing-suit, drinks by the pool, social media days are over. It isn't fair. It isn't fun. But teachers are held to a different standard than many other professionals. Watch the news and read newspapers, when teachers get in trouble, even when it has nothing to do with school, their profession isn't just mentioned later in the article. No. It is the headline: "Teacher does _____" It doesn't matter what goes into the blank, teachers are teachers first in the eyes of the parents and the community.

Part of this is: teachers help shape young minds, and with such a lofty job title comes an expectation of super-human proportions. Part of it is: many teacher salaries are funded through tax-payer money, and the impression in the community is that teachers are providing a service to the community. None of this is right. None of it is fair. And all of it matters.

You can still go out to the beach. You can still have a drink at a restaurant. You can still go to birthday parties and movie nights and wine tastings. You can still have a life. You just need to censor your social media pictures, whether you post the pictures yourself or someone else tags you. Your profile should also be private, and you should never accept friend invitations or follows from parents or students (once they graduate, if they seek you out, it is fine to accept them—but don't seek *them* out. That might seem creepy).

Censoring social media does have to do with your lifestyle and your hobbies, but it also has to do with your politics and opinions. This is true of many jobs, but teaching is a profession requiring benign profiles, ones not filled with party lines or propaganda. Teachers need to be careful what they like, what they share, and who they follow—even if their profiles are private. One "friend" can take a screenshot with the potential to ruin a career.

Table 63.1 is a list of what to avoid on your social media account as you prepare to enter the teaching field (because yes, they will most likely search for you before or after the interview).

Table 63.1

Avoid	Do This Instead
• Bathing suit photos (unless there is a LOT of skin covered—this goes for both men and women) • Obvious drinking (get rid of the red plastic cups) • Any post supporting or promoting hate of any kind • Liking or following extremist groups • Being overly critical of any one person or group of people on your social media • Engaging in drama or name calling on social media • Badmouthing the school district or school • Talking about students or parents, even if their names aren't mentioned • Smoking or illegal drug use (but really, avoid this in life, too, not just on social media)	• Wear a cover-up in pictures where you are in a bathing suit. • If you are drinking, pour it into a nondescript cup (and do not be blatantly drunk in the picture). • Promote love and acceptance every chance you get. • Share pictures of kittens, and "save the turtles" (nobody can hate those). • Be kind on social media (actually, everywhere). • Never talk about work on social media. • Don't list your school or school district under your profile (this is just asking for trouble. The people who really know you know where you work). • Have a tasteful profile picture in case people search your name.

None of these are hard-and-fast rules. Every community is different. However, with social media, it is best to play it safe. It isn't fair that teachers are held to a higher standard than many other professionals, but because they do have the immense privilege of helping to educate our future generations, it is best to keep the red Solo cups out of pictures.

Sixty-Four
DON'T OVERSHARE WITH YOUR STUDENTS

Hickies. There are teachers out there proudly displaying their hickies. No. There isn't a single instance where students should ever see hickies. It doesn't matter which grade level you teach, there are things that should just be covered up or avoided.

What you do in your spare time is your business—and your business only. But, you better know if you post something inappropriate to social media, kids, parents, administration, whoever, will find it. It doesn't matter that it's your private account. If your account is not private, pictures will be found. If you want to get rip-roaring drunk on Friday night, that's your business. But, the second you post something about it on a public social media account, it is no longer just your business.

If you get rip-roaring drunk at a public establishment where a parent works, or worse, a student works, that is no longer only your business.

Your students want to get to know you. And there *are* parts of your life you can show them. That's how relationships are built. And, kids have tons of questions. They see this adult, in a professional setting, who is cool and likeable and they are going to want to know how you got there and how you stay there. Students try to ask all the time about weekend hobbies. They don't need to know that some teachers like to drink while on the boat. They can know about the boat, and maybe some tubing or water skiing. But, they don't need to know you hold the rope in one hand and a White Claw in the other. They just don't need to know that part.

They can know you are married, but they don't need to know if you're having marital problems. They are not therapists, they are not adults, and most importantly, students are not your friends. There is a professional filter that must attach itself to your mouth when you are in the classroom. If you don't want to have to replay the entire conversation to the superintendent . . . or a judge . . . then don't say it in your classroom. It's simple.

Students may know you don't have kids. But they don't need to know it's because of fertility issues. Or, even worse, that you're trying. Gross.

Older students will most definitely ask you who you voted for. Avoid telling them. They do not need to know your political affiliations. You can tell them you voted. That's fair game.

How deeply you go into your personal lives will most definitely depend on the age group you teach and the climate of the school. Super conservative schools will probably have more restrictions, right? They might not want you to discuss your tattoos and the meaning behind them, although this feels like fair game in other types of schools. Unless those tattoos are in a super-secret spot, of course, because that would just be weird and inappropriate.

Teachers spend a ton of time with their kids. It could be easy to slip into a friendship-type role but that's dangerous because they are still children. It is important to remember that.

Tips to provide glimpses of your life so your students feel like they know you better:

- Show them picture of your pets.
- Show them your music playlists (if appropriate—kids love to know what kind of music their teachers listen to).
- Have a poster somewhere in your room and update it with titles once you watch a really great movie or read a really great book (school appropriate, of course).
- Tell them what college you attended.
- Tell them which sports you played.
- Show a picture of your kids.

These are small, and more importantly, appropriate gestures that let the kids have a little glimpse of your life. Relationships with students are important for learning. However, it is paramount to remember that you are a professional and they are students.

Section 13

ENDING THE SCHOOL YEAR

Sixty-Five
DON'T JUST SHOVE IT ALL IN A BOX

The last few days of school are a blissful blur of chaos. Kids are excited. Teachers are excited. There are a million things to do, and there is a deadline. Grading needs to be completely caught up. Rooms need to be cleaned. Equipment that was checked out at the start of the year needs to be turned back in. At some schools, decorations need to come off walls. Some people are moving rooms. It is a wild ride.

It can be tempting, amidst all this high-energy bedlam, to just shove all your papers in a box and deal with them next year. The temptation might also be to come back over the summer to deal with the box of papers needing to be handled. Resist. Tackle this project at the end of each year (or better yet, at the end of each quarter) and save yourself time and stress later.

There are numerous documents you are going to want to keep for next year. These might include:

- *The list of phone extensions.* Because it usually takes a bit for a new one to be developed, and if you need to call someone day one of next year, you will want that list.
- *Your lesson plan book, or spreadsheet* (or whatever it is where you recorded your lesson plans for the year). Because you think you will remember how you started the year last year . . . but you won't. Not entirely.
- *Handouts that were helpful for both you and the kids.* There is no reason to re-create the same document next year. Save that sucker (and even if you have it electronically, computers crash. Having one physical copy isn't a bad idea).
- *Student final exams.* Save these until around October of the next school year. This protects you and the students in case there is an error in the transcript somewhere and a student needs to contest a grade.
- *ESE, IEP documents.* Same time frame. Shred these around October of the next school year.
- *A roster of your students' names.* You might want to use it to jot down standardized testing scores as they come in. It is nice to see it on one page so you can reflect on the progress your kiddos made last year and reflect on your teaching strategies.

- *Sweet notes from your kiddos or parents.* They are nice to look back on when you have a really rough day.

For as much as there is to keep, it always seems like a mini-dumpster is needed for what needs to be thrown away. Recycle or throw away the following things at the end of the year:

- *Extra copies.* You might think you will use them next year, but what a hassle. Then you have to count how many there are and double check how many more you need. You might *think* you need to store them. Unless you just operate with class-sets of some documents like tests and quizzes, the stray extra copies need to go.
- *Partially used workbooks.* Kids next year don't want the leftovers of some previous student. Plus, if names are in there at all, it could be a violation of the previous student's privacy. It is best to just start fresh. Recycle the used workbooks.
- *Student work that isn't a final exam.* If the students wanted their work, they would have grabbed it. Recycle it. Clear out your space.
- *Lessons you created that tanked.* Everyone creates them. Everyone has had a lesson flop. If it didn't go well, if you were bored or the kids were bored or it didn't yield the growth you had hoped. Get rid of it and move on. You aren't married to it just because you created (or bought) it.
- *Clean out supplies that have seen better days.* Dried-out glue sticks, markers without caps, broken crayons, the expo marker on its last legs, the dirty board eraser, pencils down to the nubs—chuck it all. A new year offers a fresh start. Treat it like one.

When you assess what is left, don't leave the "keep" pile in the box or shoved in a drawer. Organize it. Take the time to put it into files, or binders, or however you store your important paperwork. You always want to end your year strong so you set yourself up for a strong start to the following school year.

Sixty-Six
HAVE KIDS HELP

All great superheroes should have sidekicks. Crime cannot be fought single-handedly, right? Not that your classrooms are places of villainy and not to over glorify the profession or anything, but you need to utilize your kids because you can't do everything.

When it comes to cleaning the classrooms, get the kids invested in the process. You would be surprised how responsive they are when you ask for assistance. Students, even sixteen-year-old students, love to clean boards. If a sixteen-year-old is eager to clean a board, then a fifth grader might be just as eager. They'll do anything to get out of a bell ringer or exit ticket. If you hold up the eraser and say the first person to grab it doesn't have to do the exit ticket, you'll have at least four kids running for it.

Same concept applies to sweeping. If you announce that you need five minutes of sweeping and whoever does can be excluded from the bell ringer then they are all over that opportunity. In elementary school, students have roles and most kids loved it. This continues into high school, too.

If you ask one student to hang up posters outside the classroom, rarely will they say no. They like to get up and move around and you can even let them bring a friend. It would take you twice as long to get out there to hang them yourself then it would those two and you would have to wait until the end of the day when you no longer have kids. Let them do it.

At the end of the year, utilize your students the most. As you prepare your room for summer, here are some tasks you can assign them:

- *Running papers to the office* (but not ones containing sensitive information).
- *Marker testers.* Have some kids go through all the dry-erase markers and throw away the dry ones. Same with regular markers. They can test them and keep the good ones and throw away the dry ones. This is time-consuming and tedious and you certainly don't want to have to do it.
- *Organize the supplies.* At the end of the year, the colored pencils, crayons, glue sticks, etc., get all mixed up. Assign some kids to re-sort the bins.

- *Taking books off shelves so the floors can be cleaned.* Many schools have to empty the bookshelves at the end of the year. Have some kids organize your stuff into the cabinets and have some return class sets of textbooks to the book room.
- *Dusting.* You would be very surprised how many students want to use a dusting wand. They fight over it.
- *Sweeping.* Have two brooms. You can make it a competition to see who can sweep up the biggest pile in four minutes.
- *Organize the technology cart (if you have one).* You can have them dust, wipe, charge, etc.

Sometimes, especially with the older kids, they need incentives. If they can get out of an exit ticket, that usually works. But, sometimes, depending on the task, they need a bigger reward. If you don't have snacks (which always works), offer them phone time slips. These are little pieces of paper you can print out and sign. It serves as five minutes of free phone time and they can use it within your parameters. Each time they do something, they can get a slip. Some students end up with quite a few at the end of the year. They hoard them.

You will always want to check your school policy on offering incentives to your kids. But, utilize their height, their energy, and their technology know-how. Especially the technology one. You would be amazed at the technology issues these kids can solve!

Your students can be your biggest asset when organizing and cleaning your space. They use the space just as much as you do and should respect it (see the chapter about rules). With a little incentive (following district policies), you'd be surprised how much work can be taken off your plate.

Sixty-Seven

CELEBRATE WHAT WORKED

Teaching is an incredibly fast-paced profession that doesn't allow for much in-the-moment reflection. Teachers are constantly running to and from meetings and working with kids before and after school and attending parent conferences and sitting in faculty meetings and making copies and checking email and creating lesson plans and, oh yeah, teaching kids. There isn't always time to reflect. But, it is needed.

As you move into summer, the distance from the classroom can make the details of the previous school year a little fuzzy, and once you get back into school, you are programming your brain to be forward thinking and planning. You might reference student reflections that had been completed at the end of the previous year, but you also need your own reflections to look back on. If you skip this step, the opportunity for genuine reflection is lost, but this reflection is essential so mistakes aren't repeated, or so enhancements can be made to what worked.

The end of the year provides the perfect opportunity to reflect on what worked through the school year. Creating something as simple as a T-chart where one side is labeled "Worked" and the other side is labeled "Didn't Work" can be effective. As you consider what did and did not work this year, consider the following questions:

- How did my discipline policy work this year?
- How did my cell phone policy work this year?
- How did my study guides go?
- Did my tests reflect my teaching?
- Were my lessons standards based?
- Did I use my time wisely?
- What ended up being a waste of either time or resources?
- What lesson or unit went really well?
- How was my organization?

- Did I like how my desk was arranged?
- Did the seating work for the kids?
- What strategies worked best?
- Where could I use a few strategies?
- What am I proudest of this year?
- What do I, without doubt, want to repeat next year?

Based on your T-chart, you may feel like you need to drive to the local bookstore and buy Professional Development (PD) books or sign up for a conference. Remember your contract hours. Remember: the summer is your time. You are *not* obligated to go to any conferences. You are *not* obligated to read any PD books.

If you choose to read a PD book while you lay by the pool or lounge on your couch, then by all means, have at it! There are some *amazing* PD books out there (see the "For Further Reading" in the back of this book for ideas). Even if it takes you all summer to read the first three chapters of the book and you never finish it, that's OK. You will still learn something from the experience.

If you choose to go to a conference over the summer, choose wisely. If it is in a great city, go for it. If it's at a hotel with an amazing pool, go for it. If you are genuinely passionate about learning the subject of the conference, go for it. If you are dreading it, wishing you were doing something different, or if it is causing you stress in any way, stop. Don't do it. This is your summer. You are allowed to politely decline the offer of a conference. You are allowed to say no.

Don't pressure yourself to continue to be a rock-star teacher even after the kids have left for summer. You need a break, too. But remember, conference plans or not, before you leave for the summer, work on your reflection.

Feel free to take out your colorful pens and use the blank chart (table 67.1) to complete your reflection.

Table 67.1

Worked	Didn't Work

Sixty-Eight
FINANCIALLY SURVIVING THE SUMMER

There needs to be a public service announcement about how pay works over the summer months. Countless people tell teachers something along the lines of *it must be nice to have two months paid vacation.* Teachers know the truth to this. Those months are not paid vacations. Most districts stretch teacher's pay into the summer so the teachers don't starve. The hours you already put into the school year get redistributed to teachers over those few months.

Those months are grueling. Yes, teachers receive paychecks, but they are not paid for those months of not working. And, let's be real, many teachers are working their second, or even third, jobs during this time.

Different districts probably handle their summer payouts differently but many school districts provide the summer checks all up front, in May or June, and it is up to the teacher not to spend it all in one place—quite literally. It's hard not to go to a furniture store to finally replace the hot mess that sits in their living rooms. But, that can't happen, because come August, your mortgage payment needs to get paid. Oh, and groceries need to be bought, too.

There are ways to plan out the funds so they last more than the month of June. Over the years, many strategies have been tested and these three seem to work the best:

1. Set all the checks aside or in your savings account. Then, map out every two weeks on a calendar (or whenever you get paid) and then pay yourself every two weeks. This is hard to do when you have family vacations planned and want to have some extra cash, but it will help secure you in those later months.
2. Map out how much you need to set aside for bills. Calculate all your monthly expenses for June, July, and possibly even August. Set that amount aside. Then, whatever you have left over is your play-money for the summer. This can get dangerous though because you might be having a good time in June, but July and August are looking a little lackluster.

3. Pay as many bills as you can right when summer starts. If you can, pay ahead for two months, maybe even three because it might take a few weeks once school begins again to receive a paycheck.

Any route could work. However, if you have zero self-control, having that large lump sum in your account won't work for you. You probably need to operate using Option One. Options Two and Three ensure your bills are paid, which is important, but you'll be very broke by July.

Many teachers like to pick up second jobs over the summer. There are several jobs you can do that are low key and good for extra money:

- *Wait tables or bartend.* This is fast cash and can be quite lucrative, but it isn't easy.
- *Teach summer school.* But, ew. If you need the mental break then don't go this route.
- *DoorDash or any other food delivery service.* This is low commitment and easy money.
- *Uber or any other driving service.* Again, this is low maintenance.
- *Pressure washing.* You would be surprised how many people would pay for someone else to pressure wash their stuff. People always need their stuff pressure washed. Plus, how satisfying is pressure washing? You might need a business license for this though.
- *Work for a pool cleaning service.* Some vitamin D while working sounds nice.

Do whatever works for you, but it is important you find something that works. And, you need to find it quickly. The last month of summer when you suddenly realize you are out of money and it's still four weeks away from your next paycheck is terrifying. Oh! And avoid credit cards. Whatever you do, do not rely on credit cards to get you through that last month! You may tell yourself you'll pay it back with your first check. You won't. It's a trap.

Set yourself up so you don't start the next school year stressed out over money. Although you may not have that new purse or those new golf clubs you wanted back in June, you'll have groceries. You'll thank yourself.

FOR FURTHER READING

Teach Like a Pirate: Increase Student Engagement, Boost Your Creativity, and Transform Your Life as an Educator by Dave Burgess (2012).

Become an Effective Teacher in Minutes: Best Teaching Practices You Can Use Now by Marjan Glavac and Adam Waxler (2019).

Tools for Teachers: Practical Tools and Tips to Improve Classroom Management by Prana Thoppil (2018).

Tools for Teaching: Discipline, Instruction, Motivation—Primary Prevention of Classroom Discipline Problems by Fred Jones (PhD Fredric H. Jones, Patrick T. Jones, and Jolynne Jones) (2014).

ABOUT THE AUTHORS

Heather Garcia has her BA in English, her MA in English, and an MFA in Writing and has taught courses ranging from elementary-level art, full of fingerpaint and clay modeling to high school remedial reading and writing to Advanced Placement Literature. She was also a professor at Florida Gulf Coast University teaching composition to incoming freshmen and sophomores, which are really just older high school students with a bit more freedom. She has trained new and experienced teachers in new educational programs at her district and she has been a mentor for new teachers for over ten years.

Her current teaching assignment has extended to her coaching and mentoring middle and high school teachers from across the district as an English curriculum and instruction specialist. She models lessons with students, helping fill gaps and demonstrate practical classroom management and instructional styles, and she works closely with new and striving teachers as they navigate the nuances of teaching. She also coaches veteran teachers who have new teaching assignments or need engaging new lessons. She has taken what she has learned in the classroom over the past seventeen years and presented educational practices at various state and national level educational conferences, all in the hopes of helping new and veteran teachers reignite a passion for whom and what they teach.

Michelle Lindsey has her BA in English and Literature and her MFA in Writing and has a wide range of teaching experience. After earning her AA, she became a substitute teacher at a small charter school to enhance her teaching experience while finishing college. After obtaining her BA and moving into a full-time position at a public high school, her first full-time position was almost her last when she barely survived her first year of teaching. She was convinced to take over for a remedial English II teacher who suddenly and tragically passed away in the middle of the year. With the support of her sister, Heather, she made it through that first year and now, almost a decade later, teaches a variety of grades from 9–12 and from classes ranging from remedial English to AICE (Advanced International Certificate of Education) Cambridge courses and AP Seminar, AP Research, and AP Literature with some debate and speech sprinkled into the mix. She also became the state of Florida's representative for the High School Teacher of Excellence Award offered by NCTE in 2020.

Michelle has various publications ranging from flash fiction to essays. She currently is the program planner for the English department at her public high school, serves on her school's literacy committee to help promote active reading and better writing throughout all disciplines within her school, and her district's curriculum mapping committee. She also mentors new and veteran teachers coming into the district. She has presented at state and national conferences where she highlights the importance of student engagement with effective teaching techniques.

www.ingramcontent.com/pod-product-compliance
Lightning Source LLC
Chambersburg PA
CBHW021759230426
43669CB00006B/124